Coming
of Age

Coming of Age

African American Male Rites-Of-Passage

Paul Hill, Jr.

Cover illustration by Harold Carr

Photo credits:
    William Hall
    Paul Hill, Jr.
    Joel Warren (back cover photo)
  First edition, first printing

Copyright 1992 by Paul Hill, Jr.

African American Images
Chicago, Illinois

Table of Contents

DEDICATION

I would like to dedicate this book to the Creator, my ancestors, my wife, Marquita and children (Greer, Courtney, Jason, Antar, Fanon, Mara, Raina, and Maren). Also, I would like to dedicate this book to Raymond Martin (Moun), Joseph Hawkens (Hawk-Man), and other fallen warriors who are no longer with us.

ACKNOWLEDGEMENT

I would like to acknowledge the following individuals and organizations for their pioneering scholarship, practice, and support of Rites-Of-Passage and Transformation Models for African American youth:

PIONEERS
Molefi Asante
Frank Fair
Reuben Harpole
Maulana Karenga
Kujuliwa Kennedy
Jawanza Kunjufu
Linda Meyers
Wade Nobles
Anyim Palmer
Useni Perkins

MENTORS
Hannibal Afrik
Anthony Mensah

ACKNOWLEDGEMENT

SUPPORTERS

African American Mens Leadership Council

Goldie Alvis
The Cleveland Foundation

George Ashley

Roy Bernard
Cincinnati Rites Organization

Creigs Beverly

Elbert Clark
East End Neighborhood House

Jerome Cargile

Fran Frazier
Ohio Dept. of Human Services

Donald Freeman
League Park Center

Barbara Galloway
Cuyahoga County Dept. of Human Services

The Kellogg Foundation

Mariba Kelsey
The Ohio Africentric Rites-Of-Passage Network

The Ohio Rites-Of-Passage Network Youth and Adults

Sojourner Truth Adolescent Rites Society

GRIOTS

Tom Puryear

Preston Wilcox

INTRODUCTION

The African American male has been labeled as dangerous, obsolete, endangered, and at risk. Much of who the African American male is has been externally determined by the circumstances of our Western existence—White male supremacy.

Coming Of Age: The African American Male Rites-Of-Passage provides an overview of the issues confronting the African American male and a strategy to nurture a new generation of African American males. The four-chapter book is diagnostic and prescriptive. Chapters One and Two focus on the following questions:

♦ What is the social status and the new demographics of the African American male?

♦ What external threats are devastating the African American male and the African American community?

11

- What is society's definition of manhood?
- What happens to African American men who accept society's definition of manhood, but are denied the resources to demonstrate their masculinity through traditional channels?
- What are Rites-Of-Passage and Africentricity?

Chapters Three and Four focus on the following questions:

- What is the nearest equivalent to ancient initiation rites? What is the difference between the old and new?
- Throughout Africa, what are the ten basic principles of educating and socializing African children?
- What is an example of a Rites-Of-Passage process and how does it function?
- What are the foundations of Rites-Of-Passage?
- What is institutionalization?
- What is the relationship between Rites-Of-Passage and socialization?
- How can Rites-Of-Passage become a way of life?

Coming Of Age: The African American Male Rites-Of-Passage was written out of concern for the collective welfare of the African American community; however, the book specifically focuses on the male. Rites-Of-Passage is presented as a coming of age strategy for males which is necessary for their survival.

This is a work which is both reactive and proactive. It is reactive in that it represents a response to the cumulative forces currently operating in the

United States, which if not abated, will give truth to the statement, "Black males in the United States are endangered". The convergence of these forces, inclusive of but not limited to, homicide, suicide, imprisonment, infant mortality, AIDS, alcohol, drugs, toxic waste, and cardiovascular disease all have the net effect of hastening the demise of Black males. It is a proactive work in that it calls upon the collective consciousness, will, knowledge, and creativity of the Black community to institutionalize Rites-Of-Passage as part of the socialization process for rearing male children in a society hostile to their presence and committed to their destruction.

Brought here on slave ships to work, Black men are no longer needed to work in America.

We have more African American males in prison than college.

Homicide is the leading cause of death for young Black men.

CHAPTER ONE

Endangered African American Men

Strong Men
Sterling Brown

Strong men getting stronger is, in the vernacular, 'The Bottom Line.'

In recent years, considerable attention has been given to the dominant role assumed by males in the United States. Because of the way mainstream society is structured, it is argued that males receive an unfair share of its benefits. However, for Black males, the so-called advantage does not exist. Few things in America are more hazardous to an African American male than assuming a masculine role. Given this view of the African American male status, the following quote from psychiatrist Alvin Poussaint is even more significant:

> No one can deny that being a Black man in America is a high-risk adventure. The social and health status of the Black male is alarming. The life expectancy at birth is about sixty-four years for Black men, seventy years for White men, seventy-three years for Black women, and over seventy-seven years for White women. Black males have higher age-adjusted death rates for cancer, heart disease, cirrhosis of the liver, strokes, accidents, and lung disease than White males, White females and Black females. The leading cause of death among young Black men has become Black-on-Black homicide. And significantly, about forty-five percent of police killings in recent years have been of Black men, who are in general, frequent victims of police brutality. The suicide rate of young Black males has more than doubled since the 1960's and is more than four times the suicide rate of a comparable group of Black females.[1]

Poussaint's statement describes the African American male experience as one that is "life-threatening" and "psychologically brutalizing." These circumstances have crippling consequences for the mental health of the families of African American males and on the quality of life in Black communities. When the well-being of African American males is threatened, the entire African American community is at risk.

IMAGES OF AFRICAN AMERICAN MEN

Conferences, media specials, commissions, and reports have focused on the condition of Black males. The 1985 premiere of *The Color Purple*, the 1986 CBS Special, *The Vanishing Black Family*, and the 1987 South African-produced mini-series, *Shaka Zulu* presented negative images of African American males. The crisis, dilemma, peril, and images of African American males have been externally created to deny them wholeness and greatness as the first men to walk the Earth.

Black men were stolen from Africa as whole people with a strong self-concept, cultural competence, high self-esteem, positive behavior, and group loyalty. However, through physical enslavement and the current chains and images of psychological enslavement, many Black men are now fragmented and fractured males characterized by a confused self concept, cultural incompetence, ambivalent behavior, depreciated character, adaptive behavior, confused group loyalty, and reactionary behavior. As psychologist Naim Akbar says in his book, *Chains and Images of Psychological Slavery,* "The historical images which we have inherited continue to sabotage many of our efforts for true manhood and womanhood."

The nature of American society has traumatized African American males. Not only has the environment contributed to the physical death of many African American males, it has also contributed to the psychological death of many more. Two literary classics that characterize the effects of American society on the African American male are Ralph Ellison's *Invisible Man*[2] and Richard Wright's *Native Son*[3].

The socioeconomic institutions of the American society have developed techniques for systematically making a large percentage of African American males useless in fulfilling their family obligations. African American males have had a difficult time protecting themselves from the pressures of major institutions in society. These institutions have resulted in negative consequences for family relationships in African American communities.

In order to cope and survive in their environment, it has become necessary for human beings to react through adaptation. African American males have had to incorporate adaptive values and mechanisms to survive the disabling impact of devalued status. However, the evolution of the adaptive process to insulate the African American male population from the consequences of social stress has created a Catch-22 effect. The adaptation to one aspect of the environment has precluded his effective utilization of other aspects of the environment which are essential sources of sustenance. This adaptive process has resulted in increasing insulation and isolation in personal-social interactions, alienation from those institutions and affiliations which have traditionally provided stabilizing points of reference, and diminished faith in nature, community, family, authority, and in oneself as continuing influential forces. The protective adaptation of the African American male personality to the rigors of the increasingly oppressive social environment has resulted in his isolation from essential sources of support for personal and spiritual survival.

When it comes to explaining why the African American male is removed from the civilian population at a much higher rate than that of his non-

Black counterparts, many sociologists and psychologists argue that it is the direct result of years of negative socialization. America has always defined the male role as that of protector and provider, but for a number of reasons, the African American male is frequently incapable of playing that role. While he may understand that racism is frequently the cause of his failure, the African American male's structural inability to play his role can take a psychological toll and may lead to violence.

Definitely, not all African American males have been cruelly affected by the forces I have presented, but few can claim complete immunity. It is clear that the eradication of these forces or their neutralization, will require a radical rearrangement of societal institutions with a corresponding change at the very core of America's value system. This need for change will call for a protracted struggle, as those whose vested interests are secured through maintaining the devalued status of African American males will not voluntarily give up their privileged positions.

THE FEAR OF OVERPOPULATION

To maintain their privileged positions, those who feel threatened will use any means necessary to protect their vested interests. Such a threat is perceived relative to the high fertility rate of people of color in America and throughout the world. Industrial nations feel it is not in their best interest to allow the increasing worldwide birth rates of people of color to continue. Overpopulation hysteria is both philosophically and politically congenial to the outlook of those who see the world's problems consist-

21

ing of foolish people needing direction by the wise.[4]

Many Western officials and intellectuals are likewise calling for strong leadership to control population growth in less-developed countries. This leadership almost invariably means various degrees of authoritarianism wielded by the Westernized elite through the World Health Organization and World Bank against the general populace. Africa has the world's highest birth rate averaging forty-four births per one thousand people, as reported in 1987 by The Worldwatch Institute, an independent population reference bureau. Asia, not including China, has the second highest birth rate at thirty-three per one thousand people while Latin America has a rate of thirty.[5]

While the developing world struggles with too many people, the large industrial nations face the opposite problem, so few babies that their populations may begin to shrink. The United States averages sixteen births per one thousand while Canada has a birth rate of fifteen. Europe has the lowest birth rate at thirteen per one thousand people.[6]

In 1986, one of every ten babies born in the United States is the offspring of a mother who came from another country. Fifty-three percent of foreign-born mothers were from Latin America, the largest share from Mexico. Native-born women averaged 67.5 births per one thousand, while the rate was 98.9 for women born elsewhere. Leading were Mexico natives, with 141.9 births per one thousand, compared with 90.4 for women from the balance of Latin America. The rate for Asian women was 104.8 and it was 54.2 for those from Europe.[7]

Within the United States, after a period of sus-

22

tained growth, the nation's youth population is shrinking. Between 1975 and 1995, the number of young people aged sixteen to twenty-four is expected to decline from 35 million to 29 million or from twenty-three percent to fifteen percent of the population. However, this smaller youth population will consist increasingly of Black and Brown youngsters. In 1950, less than fifteen percent of those eighteen and under were non-White; today, the figure is thirty-six percent and growing.

The new demographics show that African Americans, who currently make up eleven percent of the work force, will account for almost one-fifth of all labor force entrants in the years ahead. The nation will have fewer youngsters than in the past and more of them will be Black and Brown.[8] These facts have important implications for nearly all of our major institutions, among them the Military and the Social Security System. The nation's rapidly aging White middle-class will draw its retirement income from an increasingly Black and Hispanic work force. The nation's defense will depend increasingly on Blacks and Browns in uniform.

POPULATION CONTROL: AIDS AND ADDICTION

What has America and the industrial nations' response been to the population shifts and changing world economy? Of the fifty million people worldwide believed to be infected by the deadly AIDS virus, ninety-seven percent are of African descent. Thirty million or sixty percent live in sub-Saharan Africa. In this country, there are an estimated two million carriers of the virus. African Americans and Hispanics comprise forty percent of the victims who have AIDS, although they represent just twenty percent of the population. The Surgeon General, in his 1986 findings, reported that fifty-five percent of all infants with AIDS are African American.[9]

In the 1990's, it is not at all inconceivable that persons with the same mindset and psychological orientation that conducted the Tuskegee syphilis experiments on unsuspecting African American men and their families for a period of forty years (1932-1972) would not go further and develop a deadly disease that could be spread among people of color and other undesirable population groups, again for the purpose of a systematic depopulation agenda.

Other external threats to the African American community are drugs, alcohol, and toxic waste. African Americans did not become a public part of the drug abuse scene in any significant fashion until the 1950's and 60's. Even then, there are several plausible explanations. The pre-World War II migration of African Americans to Northern urban cities created larger, concentrated pockets of African Americans. Alcohol has always been available to the poor, particularly rural poor, who learned how to make it themselves.

Perhaps the most powerful, yet least spoken about factor, was the shift in channels of heroin distribution. There was a deliberate infestation of addictive narcotics into the African American urban community in the early 1950's. This was a calculated effort to exploit the psychological vulnerability of an uprooted and unstable population and to create a dependency on a commodity by external criminal forces. As a result, the crime rates in these areas skyrocketed and the number of African Americans, particularly males, identified as known users became a very disproportionate part of the statistical data nationally. Black-on-Black criminal behavior began to climb along with the increased drug usage.

Black males, particularly the young in urban areas, have clearly been a vulnerable group in relation to drugs. Homicide is the leading cause of death for young Black men and ninety-five percent of the victims are killed by other Blacks.[10] Cities such as Detroit, Los Angeles, New York and Washington D.C. have become inundated with children's funerals because of the heavily-armed youth gang involvement with drugs. A significant number of Black AIDS victims in the United States are intravenous drug users. Black males accounted for twenty-three percent of the 22,648 male cases and Black women accounted for fifty-one percent of the 1,634 female cases of AIDS reported in 1986.[11] Of the total United States pediatric AIDS cases, eighty-two percent were born to Black females.[12] The majority of these cases were intravenous drug users who resided in New York and New Jersey.

Alcoholism is now perceived as one of the most significant health, social, and mental health problems within the Black population. The consequences of alcohol abuse . . . have been extreme for Black Americans, especially Black males.[13] The links between alcohol abuse and physical violence have been extreme for Black Americans, particularly males. These problems include homicides, accidents, criminal assaults, and other run-ins with the law.

Young Black males are being bombarded with

Black entertainers' promises of fulfillment through liquor. Even though studies have shown that some sixty percent of homicides in the Black community are alcohol-related, Black communities are plastered with billboards extolling the virtues of alcohol. The African American community is also flooded with massive liquor advertising campaigns that underwrite the celebration of Black History Month, provide scholarships and sponsor community events—from schoolyard basketball tournaments to the annual meeting of the Congressional Black Caucus.

Three liquor stores in Cleveland (Ohio) that primarily serve a desperately impoverished segment of the Black community, had combined earnings of $3.7 million in liquor sales in 1986. That was nearly equal to the combined packaged liquor sales of all stores in two neighboring counties, which together have a population base nearly six times that of the Cleveland area and an average per-capita income (1986) that was more than three times as high.[14]

A 1987 national report by The Commission for Racial Justice documented that forty percent of the nation's total commercial hazardous waste landfill capacity was located in three predominately Black and Hispanic communities. There are ten metropolitan areas where more than ninety percent of the Black population lived in areas with uncontrolled toxic waste sites; Memphis, St. Louis, Houston, Cleveland, Chicago, Atlanta, Seattle, New York, Buffalo, Oklahoma City.[15] Cancer Alley, an 85-mile stretch between Baton Rouge and New Orleans along the Mississippi River has 136 chemical companies and refineries. This area, which is occupied by a majority of poor Black people, has the highest incidence of lung cancer in the world.[16]

The external threats, i.e., AIDS, drugs, alcoholism and toxic waste have been compounded by internal problems. Internal problems related to self-destructive behaviors and deviant lifestyles have been manifested in the breakdown of families and community disorganization. The behavior and lifestyles contributing to family breakdown and community disorganization are rooted in an environment of I-ism. I-isms flourish in the midst of an overall decline in the quality of reference group life. Self-preservation overrides group preservation, when in reality there can be no self-preservation without group continuation. This disengagement of self from group interest is more likely when one is unable to recognize the ways in which life can be infused with a sense of meaning and thereby increase social value. Groups which are preoccupied with mere survival fail to establish long-term development agendas, agendas which by their very existence give direction, meaning, and purpose to individual behavior. Agendas target redemption milestones, direct productive energies, reduce role, place, and value ambiguities and provide the evaluative framework in which it is possible to determine how well a group has survived.

The experience of European Jewry is a classic example of the meaning and significance of a coherent, group-oriented agenda. After the Holocaust, the expression among Jews "Never Again" became the rallying cry for all Jews, liberal and orthodox alike. It was and is an expression which reflects the need for prescriptions and actions necessary to create permanent safeguards against the recurrence of death camps. The following seven principles outline the Jewish agenda designed to

27

ensure that a holocaust never occurs again:

1. The placement of responsibility on the Jewish family as the central unit for transmitting the values and beliefs which give meaning to Jewish life and which accentuate its social value.

2. An insistence on the non-negotiable right for Israel to exist.

3. Enforcement of educational excellence.

4. Developing occupational skills which lessen Jewish dependence on others and makes others more dependent on them.

5. An unfaltering religious/spiritual orientation.

6. An unequaled domestic/international intelligence network.

7. A manhood development process for boys.

Adherence to this prescriptive agenda has permitted the Jewish community to overcome the destructive confines of survivalism and clearly has equipped it to sustain, develop, and prevail.

Many are aware of the six million Jewish people who died as a result of the Holocaust—a great human tragedy; yet how many are aware of the number of Africans who died as a result of the Middle Passage? Historians differ in their projection that between thirty and one hundred million African people died before ever reaching these shores. The Atlantic Ocean is literally paved with the remains of captured African people—a great human tragedy.

Based on the continuing holocaust of African Americans, the author is unaware of any similar set of principles and plan which the African American community has agreed upon and adopted to serve as its reminder of "Never Again."

AFRICAN AMERICAN MEN: VICTIMS OR VICTIMIZERS

The vulnerability of the African American community has resulted in an exploited population of children, women, and elders. The irony of such a situation is that the African American male is a victim and victimizer. He has assumed and internalized certain societal traits associated with masculinity, dominance, competitiveness, and aggressiveness. The internalization of such traits are conflicting. Males are in conflict with themselves, other males, their mates, and children.

The Western male seasoning process has placed males at risk. The process is related to machoism and a privileged sex image. American males are raised by females to play a role of lover - husband - parent - breadwinner - strong - and - silent - male. These impossible demands psychologically cripple and eventually, physically kill males.

What is a man? Herb Goldberg in his book, *Hazards of Being Male*, comments:. . . an independent strong achiever who can be counted on to be always in control. His success in the working world is predicated on the repression of self and display of a controlled, deliberate, calculated, manipulative responsiveness. The man who feels, becomes inefficient because he gets emotionally involved and this inevitably slows him down and distracts him. His more dehumanized competition will then surely pass him by.[17]

Male seasoning thus becomes a dehumanization process of indoctrinating you against yourself; a conspiracy designed to make you a zombie, with no feelings and compassion for your children, women, or brothers.

A central question to comprehending the behavior and attitudes of African American men in America is: What happens to African American men who accept society's definition of manhood, but are denied the resources to demonstrate their masculinity through traditional channels? An awareness of this precarious predicament is key to understanding the unique psychological and social drudgery which distinguishes African American men from other sex/race groups in America. While objectively, the economic position of African American women is worse than that of White men, White women, and African American men, subjectively it is African American men who are forced into the humiliating "double bind" of proving their manhood while being denied access to the legitimate tools with which to do so. The hopes, aspirations, attitudes, and behaviors of African American men are formed in this process of masculine attainment and its vicissitudes are a major motivating force behind much of the day-to-day interactions and lifestyles of African American males.

One of the most useful theories for studying the behavioral consequences of forcing men to measure up to attainable standards of "masculinity" is suggested by the work of Robert K. Merton. According to his theory of anomie, socially-deviant or unacceptable behavior occurs in certain groups within American society because while the majority shares the basic goals of society, all do not share the means of achieving those goals. Consequently, he argues, the very structure of society actually encourages certain individuals to function deviantly to obtain its cultural goals (material and social prestige rewards of society).

Merton's five modes of adaptation that an individual can use in his adjustment to the social structure are as follows: conformity, innovation, retreatism, ritualism, and rebellion. Merton's theory describes a world that is very similar to the operation of a giant fruit-dispensing machine where the machine is rigged and some players are consistently rewarded. The deprived ones either resort to using foreign coins or magnets to increase their chances of winning (innovation), play mindlessly (ritualism), give up the game (retreatism), or propose a new game altogether (rebellion).

In American society, the ultimate resource that a male uses to demonstrate his manhood is his ability to violently exert toughness and control over others. Violence may be an effective tool for achieving what is not otherwise available to a low-status individual (such as respect and status). In brief, violence can actually be a form of social achievement. A "tough" guy's reputation can be earned in the home, streets, classroom, council/commission chambers, or corporate suites.

Males in America are socialized to conform to a code of conduct: the male role stereotype. The code/stereotype is as follows:

Act "Tough"
Acting tough is a key element of the male role stereotype. Many boys and adult males feel they have to show that they are strong and tough, that

31

they can "take it" and "dish it out" as well. You've probably run into some boys and adult males who like to push people around, use their strength, and act tough. In a conflict, these males would never consider giving in, even when surrender or compromise would be the smartest or most compassionate course of action.

Hide Emotions

This aspect of the male role stereotype teaches males to suppress their emotions and to hide feelings of fear, sorrow, or tenderness. Even as small children, they are warned not to be "crybabies." As grown males, they show that they have learned this lesson well. They become very efficient at holding back tears and keeping a "stiff upper lip."

Earn "Big Bucks"

Males are trained to be the primary and often only source of income for the family. So, males try to choose occupations that pay well and then they stick with those jobs, even when they might prefer to try something else. Males are taught that earning a good living is important, so important that a male who doesn't earn "big money" is considered inadequate in meeting society's expectations of what a "real man" should do. In fact, males are often evaluated not on how kind or compassionate or thoughtful they are, but rather on how much money they make.

Get the "Right" Kind of Job

If a boy decides to become a plumber, he will receive society's stamp of approval, for that is the right kind of job for an adult male. But if a boy decides to become a ballet dancer, many people would consider that quite strange. Boys can decide to be doctors, mechanics, or entrepreneurs without fear of trepidation, but if a boy wants to become a nurse, secretary, librarian, or kindergarten teacher, he risks being ridiculed. His friends and relatives will probably try to talk him out of his decision, because it doesn't fit the male role stereotype.

Compete Intensely

Another aspect of the male role stereotype is to be super-competitive. This competitive drive is seen not only on athletic fields, but in school and later at work. This commitment to competition leads to still another part of the male stereotype: getting ahead of other people to become a winner.

Win At Almost Any Cost

From the basketball court to getting jobs that pay the most money, males are taught to win at whatever they attempt to do. They must work, strive, and compete so that they can get ahead of other people, no matter how many personal and even moral sacrifices are made along the way to the winner's circle.

The quest for masculine attainment is not a passive adaptation to encapsulation, but a very active-sometimes devious, innovative, and extremely resistant-response to rejection and destruction. The African American male as a victimizer is a product of structural barriers that have inhibited his role as a provider-protector. Hypermasculinity, toughness, and aggressive manipulation of their environment to command respect have increased the vulnerability of the African American community. The absence of men as providers, mates, and protectors has left the African American community wide open for victimization.

In general, the collective welfare of the African American community is in jeopardy. An immediate and specific response must focus on the African American male and the issue of rearing African American male children. Such a focus must begin with conceptual framework. The conceptual framework of Africentricity as a science and method guides the writing of this book.

The germination of this perspective must be largely attributed to the research and writings of Molefi Kete Asante[18] and Linda Myers.[19] The Africentric perspective, often referred to as the Black perspective, is first and foremost a theoretical frame of reference or world view centered in Africa as the historical point of generation; unity that contains and transcends all opposites.

As a theoretical framework, it is both conceptual and pragmatic, concrete and functional. It enables one to approach feelings, knowledge, and actions as a comprehensive whole rather than as disparate segments. It enables one to move from a position characterized by a neo-colonial mentality to one of relative autonomy. Relative autonomy refers to the functional need to acknowledge one's fundamental accountability to one's community, as well as to oneself, thereby avoiding the inapplicable perspective of Western individualism.

Two important elements make up the Africentric perspective: (1) its assessment-explanatory power and (2) its functional power. Assessment-explanatory power means screening out aspects of African American life and experience in terms of healthy or

34

unhealthy implications. In using the Africentric perspective to screen reality, one is able to predict the behavior and consequences of the elements which make up reality. Assessment-explanatory power also reveals historical and contemporary feeling tone in past and present experiences of African American people. The functional power of the Africentric perspective is directive in that it gives guidance and purpose to the thoughts and actions of African American people. It is not anti-White or reactionary, nor is it a defensive strategy; it is an offensive (unifying) strategy that is pro-Black.

The Africentric perspective, grounded in the socio-historical struggles of African American people, forces one always to ask the alternative question. It forces one to think within a dialectical framework. For example, if African American men are disproportionately represented in the prison population, one does not assume that they commit more crimes than others. Using the Africentric perspective, the question has to be, why? That question forces the analysis beyond the consideration of individual and/or personal pathology.

Paramount in the Africentric perspective is that the struggles of African Americans have historically had the central goal of gaining some measure of human dignity in a society which too often disregards the culture of non-Western peoples. Africentricity promotes an appreciation for, and utilization of, the collective experiences of Black people in every dimension of existence.

In writing on the Black experience, Leon Chestang defined three socially-determined and institutionally-supported conditions which are endemic in the African American experience: Social injustice, societal inconsistency, and personal importance. He says that to function in the midst of any one of these does cruel and unusual violence to the personality. To live as "Black men do," constrained by all three, subjects the personality to severe crippling and even destruction.[20]

One who uses the Africentric perspective is rarely content with the notion that "what is" is what ought to be, or "what ought to be" is not achievable. It provides hope in the midst of despair, courage when threatened by terrorism, belief in the midst of doubt, the will to overcome against staggering odds, perseverance despite fatigue, and the strength to "hold on" when there is little on which to hold. A perspective is not, as most Western scholars have assumed, an aspect of culture independent of subject matter or content. Such distinctions attempt to fragment phenomena that cannot be fragmented without being misunderstood and unappreciated.

One must accept the African perspective as an integral component of African American culture that is manifested (though not to the same degree) in all aspects of African American life. An understanding of this uniquely Africentric world view provides the key to identifying those elements in African American life and culture which are distinctively African and using those differences to define principles for socializing African American male children. Purposeful and constructive transformational strategies will then emanate from those principles.

Our youth hang on corners because adults do not provide alternatives.

For the first time, we are facing a generation that will not surpass the educational attainment of the generation that spawned it.

CHAPTER TWO

The Deterioration Of African American Men

Gabriel Mistal

> *We are guilty of many errors and many faults, but our worst crime is neglecting the fountain of life. Many of the things we need can wait, the child cannot.*

Seventeen-year-old Michael W. Turner was sentenced 66 to 255 years in jail after pleading guilty to brutal crimes against thirty people over a ten-month period of time. Turner, an admitted crack user, dropped out of school in the seventh grade and had been living on the streets for about four years. He

39

cannot read or write. His only visitor during five months in County Jail was his lawyer.

A sixteen-year-old youth, Jacques Broussard, strangled a teenage girl named Marcy Conrad. When his friends thought he was only boasting about the killing, he took them to see the body. None of them told their parents and only one finally went to the police.

Seventeen-year-old David Santos has lived the last three and a half years of his life in a secured detention facility where minors tried as adults are sent. According to the District Attorney, since age ten, David has been arrested thirty-eight times on a variety of charges including: weapon possession, narcotics possession, car theft, a number of robberies, and two homicides. David Santos is an intelligent, articulate, perceptive youth, but he is also a youth who by age thirteen had killed his first person and who has killed at least once again since then.

Michael, Jacques, and David represent an ever-increasing alienated group of African American male youth. The indifference, alienation, disrespect for self and others is present in a growing number of male youth who are faced with inadequate schools, poverty, family breakdown, community disorganization, and unemployment.

Today, African Americans have less effective controls over the practices of childrearing and the education/socialization of its youth than ever before. The by-products of this loss are the first generation of Blacks without strong ties to the church or to the South. They are the first to be so profoundly integrated into the life and values of White America.

Social control of our children has been lost to the

state, on one level, to the volatile and quixotic peer group, and the dictates of popular culture and group acceptance on the other. On a higher plane, the agencies of nurturance and development (the family, religious institution, and school) have all but relinquished the duties of discipline and responsibility for child guidance to the agencies of punishment and rehabilitation, i.e., the courts, judges, police, and professional correctors, such as counselors and psychotherapists.

Within the last thirty years, much has happened to family structure. In 1950, the home had the greatest impact on children, followed closely by school, church, peer group, and television. By 1991, the peer group had moved into first place, followed by the media, school, family, and religious institutions.[1] Family breakdown and community disorganization, along with the increasing influence of the streets and electronic media, have created youth who exhibit interpersonal violence and self-destructive behavior.

THE GLAMORIZATION OF DRUGS AND VIOLENCE

Glamorization of drugs and violence and the easy availability of handguns has resulted in a fuse that was ignited in the 1960's and continues in the 1990's. The increase in youth street gang activities has exploded across the nation. "Week by week and year by year, the ominous statistics mount up: In 1987, when gang homicides rose to 387 in Los Angeles County, the police made more than twelve thousand gang arrests. The Los Angeles Police and Sheriff's Departments estimated seventy thousand gang members in Los Angeles County."[2]

Dangerous as it is, the situation on the West Coast is just part of a much larger problem. Big-city gangs in New York, Chicago, Miami, and Washington, D.C. have broken into the crack business and some are actively spreading drugs and violence to other cities all across the country. In Chicago, gang membership has reached an estimated thirteen thousand. "Today's Black street gangs are more volatile, more destructive and more criminally-oriented than their predecessors." [3] Due to the saturation of drugs in the Black community, Black street gangs have organized a network of drug trafficking that generates high profits which they are not willing to relinquish. And because of the hopelessness and despair that fester in the Black community, they have more than a sufficient number of consumers to support this lucrative enterprise.

When people have little hope and are immersed in despair, drugs become a highly marketable product. Contrary to what occurred during the 1960's, when Black street gangs became the victims of drugs, Black street gangs are now the victimizers. Today, there are large percentages of Black street gangs who are not hooked on drugs. They realize drug addicts are often unmanageable and unpredictable. In summary, the factors contributing to the resurgence of youth street gangs are the increased flow of drugs in the Black community, joblessness, and poverty.

A TROUBLING ECONOMY

African American youth, males in particular, are being programmed for self-destruction. The increases in teenage homicides and suicides reflect the extent of their detachment, alienation, and lack of identity. Our children, the hope of the future, are in trouble. Where are African American males in America?[4] The Black teen male population, age thirteen to nineteen, comprises 7.7% of the total Black population and 16.3% of the total Black male population. The Black teen male, like the Black United States population in general, is concentrated in the South. The regional breakdown as of 1980 was:

Northeast 17.9%
North Central 19.5%
South 54.1%
West 8.5%

Most Black teen males can be found in urban (83.2%), as opposed to rural (16.8%), settings. Of the Black teen males age fifteen to nineteen in urbanized areas, three-fourths can be found in the central cities (74.2%), while one-fourth reside in the suburbs or "urban fringe" (25.8%). Close to one-third of all deaths of Black teen males age fifteen to nineteen are homicides (31.0%). Contrary to popular belief, the overwhelming majority of Black teen males age fifteen to nineteen live within a family (97.2%). While a large percentage of Black teen males age fifteen to seventeen live with both parents (44.1%), an equally large percentage reside with only one parent (46.4%). The breakdown with respect to the living arrangement for Black teen males is:

Living with both parents 44.1%
Living with mother only 41.8%
Living with father only 4.6%
Living with neither parent 9.5%

Data indicates that African American males bear the brunt of the inequities in the American social, economic, education, and health systems. The results have crippling consequences for our families and communities. The privileged status males have in the mainstream result of institutional sexism have been canceled out due to our racial subordination as African American males. Race continues to be an important variable for understanding the role of African American men in society.

A man's worth in America has been based on his ability to provide. We, whose ancestors provided two hundred and forty years of free labor to build America, have outlived our usefulness. As a people whom the society has always denied social value, we have also lost economic value. Our purpose to this society has ceased to be a compelling issue. Once an economic asset, we are now considered an economic burden. The wood is all hewn, the water all drawn, the cotton all picked, and the rails reach from coast to coast. The ditches are all dug, the dishes are put away, and only a few shoes remain to be shined. Thanks to old Blacks and new machines, the chores of the nation are done. Now, we face a society that is brutally pragmatic, technologically advanced, deeply racist, and surly. In such a society, the absence of social and economic value is a crucial factor in anyone's fight for a future.[5]

Meaningful employment provides the foremost social linkage between existence and acceptance as a worthy person in the eyes of others. Employment provides the measure of a man; to be out of a job is simply to be out of American society. Social effectiveness, citizenship, even self-respect depend on access to a job. Without a job, a man ... cannot possibly be socially effective. He is deprived of citizenship, of social standing, of the respect. No amount of economic relief can possibly offset the social destruction of chronic unemployment.[6] Frederick Douglass emphatically informed the readers of his newspaper, "We tell you to go to work; and to work you must go or die. Men are not valued in this country, or in any country, for what they are; they are valued for what they can do. It is vain that we talk about being men, if we do not do the work of men."[7] Both joblessness and race intimidate our existence. When one does nothing, the threatening question arises, is one nothing? The African American male is the most vulnerable to the ravages of an unbridled and dying American capitalism.

As economic disengagement besets African Americans, we are facing for the first time in a century, a generation who will not surpass the educational or social attainment of the generation that spawned it. We, as adults, have failed our children and created walking time bombs whose minds are externally controlled. The walking time bombs are increasing in numbers. While the nation's youth population is shrinking, it is becoming increasingly Black and Brown. In 1950, less than fifteen percent of those eighteen and under were African American and Hispanic; in 1985, the figure was thirty-six percent and growing.[8] The implications of the new demographics and a changing economy are profound and challenging. The change represents both a great risk and a great opportunity. With fewer new, young workers entering the work force, employers will be hungry for qualified people and more willing to offer jobs and training to those they have traditionally ignored. At the same time, how-

45

ever, the types of jobs being created by the economy will demand much higher levels of skill than the jobs that exist today. Changes in immigration laws favoring Europeans and people from the former Soviet Union permit unbridled competition in the job market.

The rapid increase in the skills required for new jobs in the economy must be put into the context of the competence of new workers entering the work force. The evidence suggests that millions of these new workers from the United States lack even the basic skills essential for employment. For example, the recent National Assessment Of Educational Progress (NAEP), undertaken by the United States Department Of Education, found that among twenty-one to twenty-five-year olds:

> Only about three-fifths of Whites, two-fifths of Hispanics, and one-fourth of Blacks could locate information in a news article or an almanac; Only twenty percent of Whites, seven percent of Hispanics, and three percent of Blacks could decipher a bus schedule; only forty-four percent of Whites, twenty percent of Hispanics, and eight percent of Blacks could correctly determine the change due from the purchase of a two-item restaurant meal.[9]

The forces that are shaping the United States' economy will make it increasingly difficult for young African American males to succeed in the job market. African American youth, particularly males, because of miseducation, White male supremacy, family/community disorganization, and isolation are less likely to feel good about themselves. They have had unsatisfactory schooling and on-the-job training. Such problems prevent us from taking advantage of the jobs that will exist.

In the 1988-1989 school year alone, 682,000 American teenagers dropped out of school—an average of 3,789 each day.[10] In urban school districts from Boston to Los Angeles to Honolulu, up to half of all students entering ninth grade fail to graduate four years later. By the year 2000, Blacks and Hispanics (two groups dropping out and being pushed out) will compose one-third of those enrolled in public schools.[11]

Blacks and Hispanics will have a significant effect upon the economic future. In 1950, seventeen workers backed each retiree's Social Security. In 1992, just three workers back each Social Security check and one of the three is Black or Hispanic.[12] The nation's rapidly-aging White middle class will depend on an increasing African American and Hispanic labor pool to draw its retirement income. The nation's defense will depend increasingly on Blacks and Browns in uniform.

If the policies and employment patterns of the present continue, it is likely that by the year 2000, the problems of African American unemployment, crime, and poverty will be worse than they are today.

	1985 Labor Force	New Workers 1985-2000
TOTAL	115,461,000	25,000,000
Native White Men	47%	15%
Native White Women	36%	42%
Native Non-White Men (Black)	5%	7%
Native Non-White Women (Black)	5%	13%
Immigrant Men	4%	13%
Immigrant Women	3%	9%

Source: Hudson Institute

Futurists have already speculated about who will enter the work force and at what level, between now and the year 2000.[13] The problem is structural.

Preparation as fully functioning and potentially productive African American men for the future is on shaky ground. The increasing isolation of African American males from themselves, other males, and females indicates a bleak and risky future. As oppressive as our conditions were years ago, we were stronger internally as individuals and as a people. We were able to develop and sustain meaningful domestic and kinship arrangements.

Prior to 1917, over ninety percent of all African American children were born in wedlock.[14] However, in the past three decades, significant changes have taken place in the African American family. As late as 1960, eighty percent of all African American children lived with both parents but by 1990, less than fifty percent of African American children lived with two parents.

What has taken place to break the great historical continuity from Harriet Tubman to Malcolm X? Sophistication has replaced militancy. Androgyny has replaced masculinity. Me has replaced we and secularism has replaced that old-time religion.[15]

The quest for manhood in America is related to three elements of identity: As provider, protector and mate. To assume these roles has been part of the enduring struggle of African American men in America. Resistance has been the refusal of Black men to yield to the lash, lies, or racist loathing. But what does Black resistance in contemporary America mean? What does freedom mean?

Some of the confusion about manhood and womanhood lies precisely in this larger confusion about today's meaning of freedom. As a people, what are we for and what are we against? Who are our friends and who are our enemies? What is our attitude toward America and what is America's attitude toward us? All these questions were easier to answer in our past. They are more complex now. The meaning of freedom, as well as the nature of the struggle to achieve it, changes with time. When we came to America, freedom meant returning to Africa. Over the decades, it has changed from the struggle against slavery itself, to fighting against the caste system of the South and prejudice and discrimination in the North. It evolved from the struggle for civil and human rights, to the unrestricted right to vote, to Black power. Unfortunately, for some, it simply meant a good job.

BLACK MALE SUICIDE:
A PHENOMENON OR AN ESCAPE

Each generation must seek the meaning of freedom for its time and place. Yesterday's struggles and meanings of freedom are not adequate for today. Today, the meaning of freedom is the great unanswered (often unasked) question and the context of our existence is blurred, subjecting us to the interpretations and definitions of others. Being unclear leaves us open to the possibility of misdirection. Unless we understand freedom in terms other than achieving materially what our oppressors have achieved, we may be guilty of actively working toward our own demise. What we may spend a whole history struggling to obtain may prove to have little ultimate meaning. The lack of direction contributed

49

to the suicides of Volkswagen executive, William Brock, Chicago Tribune editorial board member, Leanita McClain, Cleveland School Superintendent, Fred "Doc" Holliday, and seventeen-year-old Phillips Exeter graduate, Edmund Perry. The deaths of these talented people are part of the conundrum of contemporary Black life for which we have no answers and few antidotes.

In recent years, there has been an increase in Black suicide. At one time, the national Black suicide rate was less than half that of Whites (6.0 against 12.8 per 100,000 population per year). According to the latest mortality data available, the Black suicide rate is higher than it has been in half a century. Among Black males, aged twenty-five to twenty-nine, the suicide rate nationally is greater than that of their White counterparts.

In Washington, D.C., New York, and a few other cities, the suicide rate of Black males under age thirty-five has exceeded that of their White counterparts for some time.[16] One significant racial difference in suicide patterns is that the Black suicide rate peaks in the early years, while among Whites the suicide rate increases in direct relationship to advancing age.

Self-destruction among Blacks has definitely increased and suicide among Black male youths is a particularly serious problem. Death records since 1960 show that Blacks age fifteen through twenty commit suicide at a rate higher than that of the total population of all ages.[17] The increase in Black suicides has been highest in this group and it is claimed by some behavioral scientists that if many of the Black deaths that are labeled homicide were more closely investigated, they would be revealed as suicides because the victim arranged or demanded to be killed.[18] Among fifteen through twenty-four-year-old Black males, suicide is the third leading cause of death after accidents and homicide.[19]

Several reasons have been offered for the suicide phenomenon in Black males as a group. One reason is that most Black suicide is fatalistic. Fatalistic suicide, a term originally developed by sociologist Emile Durkeim, refers to attempted and successful suicidal behaviors which are the result of severe regulation by authority figures.[20] The individual frequently feels that internal efforts are subordinate to external controls over his destiny. Many young Black males feel that human effort, planning, and volition cannot overcome the impact of schools, employers, and the police. Hence, diminished hope may lead to fatalistic suicide.[21]

What should be significant to the African American community is that most male suicide victims are killing themselves before the age of thirty-five. Just as many should be reaching the peak of their manhood, they find themselves locked in a life and death struggle with a massive and basically oppressive system of laws, customs, procedures, and enforcers. In the words of James Baldwin, "to be a Negro in this country and to be relatively conscious is to be in a rage all the time."[22]

As African American people, our behavior and actions do not reflect the behavior and actions of our ancestors. We have gone astray and lost the way. The dreams of Sojourner, Martin, and Malcolm have been betrayed by fast-talking "boys" masquerading as men. Where have all the heroes gone? Where are the African American men? If Sister Harriet Tubman was to return today, how many of us would steal away with her? Integration has resulted in assimilation, assimi-

51

lation at the expense of our wholeness, our sanity, and our children. African American leadership seems to have dwindled. Where do we go from here?

Rites-Of-Passage comes from our rich African tradition.

An initiate for Rites-Of-Passage prepares himself during his 13th birthday.

CHAPTER THREE

Cultivating A New Harvest Of Men

African Proverb | *It takes a village to raise a child.*

Our progress beyond the behavior and actions of the past will be predicated on a freedom that is self-determining. Such a freedom involves creating a new rationale, a new way of seeing, a new way of thinking, and a new way of doing! Currently, our thinking and the values which support it are Eurocentric. As victims of Western civilization, we have granted a privileged position to the values and concepts of a civilization which define us as value-less. The redefinition of freedom must be within the

perspective of our own needs and interests. There-
fore, it is of primary importance for historically
devalued, disfranchised, and oppressed groups to go
beyond our preoccupation with reacting/survival
and direct our energies to prevailing, redemption,
and development—conditions which presuppose
survival. Moving beyond a reactionary and survival
mode involves an Africentric orientation and self-
determination. The spirit of self-determination which
characterized the struggle in the 1960's is re-emerg-
ing in many areas.

A group of African American leaders in Milwaukee
recently proposed the establishment of a separate
school system for a school district in the city that is
ninety-eight percent African American with poor test
scores and has a fifty-percent dropout rate. "The
Milwaukee School System is too large and its
bureaucracy is too entrenched to allow for sufficient
change," Wisconsin State Representative Annette
"Polly" Williams recently told a Chicago newspaper.
"We just want to be given one more chance to see
what we can do with our children when we have
control."

In 1986, State Representative Melvin King and a
group of African American leaders in Boston spon-
sored a referendum calling for the secession of the
predominately African American Boston neighborhood of Roxbury from the city on the grounds that
the community's resources were being drained to
fuel Boston's economic boom with no adequate com-
pensation. The referendum was defeated by a city-
wide vote of 3-1, but it shook the Boston political
establishment.

Such self-determining efforts are necessary to
develop socially-supportive environments for Afri-

can American youth in America. The Michael Turners, Jacques Broussards, and David Santos' are products of their environment: family, church, schools, etc. The lack of control, support, values, and racial pride have created an absence of identity, purpose, and direction. Psychological and historical data support the contention that racial pride is an effective means for regulating tensions within the group. Without an Africentric orientation that promotes community power and self-determination, the need for self-reliance is eroded by a lack of values.

The 1980's and 90's will be remembered as the time when young African American men killed each other at a rate unknown anywhere else in the world. In one year alone, the Black-on-Black homicide rate was greater than the fatalities of the nine-year Vietnam War. The murder of African American boys in Atlanta also occurred in the 1980's. During this time, the child most likely to be suspended and expelled from school was the Black male child. This was also the time when the student least preferred by all teachers was the African American male student.

The value orientation of the Black Movement, during the 1960's, instilled racial pride that inspired academic success, reduced juvenile delinquency, and assisted African Americans structuring their lives for personal satisfaction. Blacks have always wanted personal power and social control, but society does not allow African Americans much access to either.

As a consequence, stress from racism is severe, without symptoms, and multifaceted. The best antidote to homicidal violence, teenage pregnancy, suicide, drugs, gangs, etc., is a pro-social effort based upon a self-image that gives a feeling of positive accomplishment and appreciation. Africentric pride promotes and enhances pro-social behavior.

Black power (ethnic pride) became a concept that captured the aspirations of the masses in issues related to community power and self-determination. This outpouring of racial pride had not been seen since the days of the Garvey Movement. Black power promoted a rich variety of ethnic thematic expressions in music, literature, theater, social sciences, symbols, and rituals. The closest contemporary parallel to the Garvey Movement was the Honorable Elijah Muhammad. Both are under-researched models that were successful in unifying large numbers of Black people.

When we can produce individuals emancipated from fears about themselves, we will produce individuals free to interact with others, free from shackles of the past, and free to prepare for a better future. All knowledge begins with self-knowledge.

A chain is only as strong as its weakest link. The chain-of-pain can be broken by producing individuals who feel good about themselves.

THE SOCIALIZATION PROCESS

Planting a harvest to break the chain-of-pain and emancipate individuals from fears about themselves must take place through regaining control over the processes of socialization. The socialization process must consist of an orderly process of maturation that prepares youth for adulthood. As referred to by Useni Eugene Perkins, *Harvesting New Generations: The Positive Development Of Black Youth*, 1985, the original harvest of African youth was contaminated by the socialization/Westernization of the slave youth process and the Negro/Black youth process. What is needed is a new harvest that reflects the Africentric (or African American) youth. The characteristic of both Negro and African American youth are as follows:

Negro/Black Youth	African American Youth
Confused self-concept	African self-concept
Cultural incompetence	Cultural competence
Ambivalent behavior	Positive behavior
Depreciated character	Transcendental character
Adaptive behavior	Self-awareness
Confused group loyalty	Group loyalty
Median/Low self-esteem	High self-esteem
Reactionary behavior	Liberated behavior

As we approach the 21st century, our people need a transformation process, a lost part of our heritage which must be restored: the Rites-Of-Passage. Adulthood training, as a phase of Rites-Of-Passage, was considered to be the most important period in a youth's life. Every boy and girl was expected to complete this training in order to be recognized as men and women. Rites-Of-Passage, as a resurrected way of thinking and doing, must become part of an ongoing socialization process.

If we are to promote the positive development of youth, we must have a transformation model that exclusively addresses their exceptional needs. The model must penetrate the racist norms which permeate this society, so youth will have the opportunity to maximize their development in spite of its adverse and debilitating influence. The model must engender values and attitudes which eradicate self-defeating behavior and replace them with liberating behavior. Rites-Of-Passage that nurtures African American males while developing liberating behavior is a step "Forward To The Past." What is Rites-Of-Passage and how can it be used?

WHY IS RITES-OF-PASSAGE NEEDED?

Today, African Americans have less effective controls over the machinery of childrearing and the education/socialization of its youth than ever before. Any group which fails to consciously and systematically frame the parameters in which these processes occur elevates the vulnerability of their young, promotes discontinuity, and worse, sets the stage for potential group demise. William Strickland notes in "Where Have All The Heroes Gone?":

> "Yet to their credit, many have not been taken in. Many do realize The Man cannot be trusted, so their moral is 'take the money and run'. But this attitude is destructive to race equity, because it produces a kind of calculating personality which believes in neither the Man nor in black people. Only self has meaning, only self is relevant. Community is simply another word for market."[1]

The middle-class perspective has its counterpart among African American street youth, where a new predator urban class has emerged. They are indifferent to and about life. They prey on the old, the innocent, and one another. The African American male youth have no productive role in the American economy and if left to this society, will never have one. Lacking historical consciousness and social conscience, they represent a great irony; they are the new warriors, only they ravage the people instead of the people's enemies.

In America, manhood is closely tied to the acquisition of wealth; wealth is the power to control others. If such a need cannot be satisfied through formal institutions via job and status, youths will seek other alternatives to compensate for denial and exclusion. In many instances, when lifelines to masculinity are systematically severed, African American males overcompensate in the sexual arena. Rape and violent acts of aggression afford a moment of power, and by extension, status.

Novelist Gloria Naylor in *The Women Of Brewster Place*, describes such a moment of power:

"These young men always moved in a pack, or never without two or three. They needed the others continually near to verify their existence. When they stood with their black skin, ninth grade diplomas and fifty word vocabularies in front of the mirror that the world had erected and saw nothing, those other pairs of tight jeans, suede sneakers, and tinted sunglasses imaged nearby proved that they were alive—they move through the streets insuring that they could at least be heard, if not seen, by blasting their portable cassette players and talking loudly. They continually surnamed each other man and clutched at their crotches readying the equipment they deemed necessary to be summoned any moment...she has stepped into the thin strip of earth that they claimed as their own. Bound by the last building on Brewster and Brickwall, they reigned in that unlit alley linked, dwarfed warrior-kings. Both with the appendages of power, circumcised by a guillotine, and baptized with the stream from a million non-reflective mirrors, these young wouldn't be called upon to fight a war in a far-off land, point a finger to move a nation, or stick a pole into the moon—and they knew it. They only had that three-hundred-foot alley to serve them as a stateroom, armored tank and executioner's chamber. So Lorraine found herself, on her knees, surrounded by the most dangerous species in existence—human males with an erection to validate in a world that was only six feet wide."[2]

The African American male's lifelines to masculinity are systematically severed. Nobody ever officially tells him when he has attained manhood and there is generally too little to signify or certify it concretely. There is no ceremony or ritual, even in Africa, to usher the African American male into proper manhood. Such a ceremony and ritual will be referred to as Rites-Of-Passage. Rites-Of-Passage are those structures, rituals, and ceremonies by which age—class members or individuals in a group successfully come to know who they are and what they are about—the purpose and meaning for their existence, as they proceed from one clearly defined state of existence to the next state or passage in their lives (Anthony Mensah).

I am of the firm belief that the clear articulation and subsequent implementation of such a process will have a measurable effect in terms of reducing, or at least minimizing, current destructive forces to

which the African American male child and man are
exposed. This belief is rooted in the understanding
that such a transformational process will have its
basis in Black objective reality. Such will factor in
the importance and implications of rearing youth in
a hostile environment and thereby provide them
with better armaments and tools with which to min-
imize the forces that would destroy them and at the
same time allow them access to the fullness of
humanity.

OLD RITES VS. NEW RITES

One of the fundamental ways human groups ensure continuity and continuation of their culture
over time, is to socialize the young in manners of
feeling, thinking, believing, and behaving so that
they become proficient bearers of the group's culture. The socialization process becomes a prescrip-
tion for group survival. It incorporates all that has
been, all that currently is, and mirrors the hope for
the future.

When comparing African American culture to
African culture, one finds in some African cultures
definite rituals which males must experience in
order to be recognized as men. These activities
prepare young people in matters of sexual life, marriage, procreation, and family/community responsibilities, while fulfilling a great educational purpose. The occasion often marks the beginning of
acquiring knowledge which is not otherwise acces-
sible to those who have not been initiated. It is an
awakening, a new day for the young. They learn to
endure hardships. They learn to live with one

another. They learn to obey. They learn the secrets and mysteries of male-female relationships.

That part of our rich African inheritance characterized by traditions of personal mastery and locus of control through the ritualization of social relationships has been lost. But, in assessing our present predicament, it is only natural that we examine our African origins to determine what it is that should have been saved. Obviously, many worthy elements of our heritage have been lost, stripped away, or simply allowed to wither. The nearest modern equivalent to ancient initiation rites is formal and institutionalized education. Both processes are compulsory. Both try to bend the unruly energies of youth to constructive social purposes. Both attempt to teach obedience, discipline, and the basics of proper behavior. Both express and communicate the central value of the sponsoring culture. The differences between the old and new are as follows:

- ♦ The old rites were religious; the new rites are usually secular.
- ♦ The old rites ran by sun and seasonal time; the new rites operate by clock and calendar, (usually sedentary and behind closed doors).
- ♦ The old rites centered on concrete experiences; the new rites rely heavily on words, numbers, and abstractions.
- ♦ The old rites were dramatic, intense, forceful, and fast; the new rites are slow, extended, and often vague about ultimate destination.
- ♦ The old rites engendered awe; the new rites commonly produce detachment and boredom.
- ♦ The old rites typically inspired participation in the ongoing history of the culture; the new

rites are often holding areas created where youth are isolated from the larger cultural reality rather than allowed to experience it.

♦ The old rites resulted in an immediate and unmistakable status change; the new rites provide no such direct deliverance into adult roles and status.

The old rites were over at a determined place and at a determined time, witnessed by the community as a whole; the new rites can go on indefinitely (dropping out and being pushed) and be severed, perhaps never resulting in general community recognition.

The old rites were in the hands of caring and concerned adults who had the interests of youths at heart; the new rites are frequently monitored by uncaring employees whose purpose for being involved is related to his or her own financial condition and interest, (a shift in the locus of control from the family to the state and corporate America).

TEN PRINCIPLES OF AFRICAN EDUCATION

Given that schools do not satisfactorily fulfill the cognitive, physical, psychological/emotional, and cultural requirements of a true Rites-Of-Passage, it is necessary for families and communities to provide a process for transition from boyhood to manhood/adulthood.

The development of a process for Rites-Of-Passage should begin with a review of African educational and socialization systems. Rites-Of-Passage does not exist in Africa and other parts of the world but is subsumed within the cultural socialization process of the community. The process is ongoing from birth to death.

The ten basic principles of African education found continent-wide for educating and socializing children are as follows:

1. *Separating child from the community and routines of daily life*
   Separation has deep spiritual meaning; it prevents distraction.

2. *Observing nature*
   African schools were built on observing nature. Cycles of growth and development are based on universal principles of life, so nature can become the teacher.

3. *A social process based on age*
   Education in Africa is a social process as opposed to the Western educational emphasis on individualism. African education is a social process conducted in groups. Observations of children indicate they learn in groups. All children are expected to master all requirements from beginning to end as a group; this is the African way. There are no gifted, average, and impaired groupings.

4. *Rejection of childhood*
   The apostle Paul said, "When I became a man, I put away childish things." A point of departure should be based on a ceremonial shift, so everybody knows it's time to quit playing and be serious.

5. *Listening to the elders*
   In African education, the most significant part is conducted by the elders. Wisdom is more

than knowledge. Young children need to be exposed to wisdom and that doesn't always mean degrees. Elders play a major role in the education and socialization of children in traditional African society.

6. *Purification rituals*
   African education is full of rituals and symbolic purifications for rebirth or change, such as baptism. Events that are symbolized are internalized and made meaningful.

7. *Tests of character*
   Via demonstrations of courage, loyalty, commitment, and persistence.

8. *Use of special language*
   New vocabulary, sounds, and symbols arc created.

9. *Use of a special name*
   Special names are uscd which are symbolic of certain characteristics. Symbols or names that have special meaning are also chosen.

10. *Symbolic resurrection*
    Upon completion of the process, one demonstrates what has happened to him by a ceremony that says, "I am now reborn into the community." The community stops its business and welcomes him back as part of the community.

Use and adaptation of the principles identified does not exclude children from a mastery of modern technology or keep them from learning about other people in the world. However, using these principles will place our children's education in a more humane light; it will also help the community go beyond the minimum requirements of mass training for employment.

RITES, RITUALS, AND REDISCOVERY

Adults are not born but made. A tree without roots cannot survive! The development of centered and whole men and women will require a rediscovery and reactivation of some of the customs, traditions, rituals, and ceremonies we have lost. Customs, traditions, rituals, and ceremonies are as veins and arteries to the body. Without connectors, there will be a breakdown in continuity. A shortage will occur somewhere in the system. Many of us have neglected even shunned these processes...at our peril. The benefits of custom, ceremonies, faith, and ritual acculturation have been discarded. This is evident in households where well-functioning males are missing; children do not have a role model or do not know what their fathers do for a living. Social scientists with a wide range of ideological and ethnic perspectives have concurred that:

> ....There is no evidence that people living in a secular urbanized world have less need of ritualized expression for their transitions from one status to another.[3]

We have been educated away from ourselves. Many educated Blacks and Whites tend to disdain education and/or socialization prescriptions for Blacks that, in some aspects, differ from those provided Whites. Blacks who have been incon-

venienced and/or denied opportunity for development are naturally afraid of anything that sounds
like discrimination or resegregation. As Afro-
Saxons, they are anxious to have anything and
everything that European-Americans have, even if it
is harmful.

What has been lacking in the socialization of
African American youth in America, is the presence
of an orderly process of maturation to prepare them
for adulthood. Institutions have failed to fill the void.
If human needs are not satisfied, human dys-
functioning will occur. Institutions are ineffective
because of their own lack of preparation and commitment to respond to the needs of African
American youth. As a result of this vacuum, most
African American youth become indoctrinated by
the streets, the electronic media, the over-glamoriza-
tion of popular culture, and the racist propaganda
that underlie American society. It is little wonder
that African American youth particularly males
have become confused, embittered, and demoral-
ized. They are walking time bombs.

If we are to promote the positive development of
African American males, we must have an
Africentric Rites-Of-Passage model that exclusively
addresses itself to their exceptional needs.
Africentric Rites-Of-Passage is a transformational
process that functions as a prelude to a metamorphosis, to manhood, to adulthood, to wholeness.
Wholeness reflects self-knowledge, personal mastery, and an Africentric locus of control. The Africentric locus of control places descendants of
Africans in the center. It proceeds on the basis of the
question, "Is it in the best interest of African
people?" Such Africentricity questions the approach

to every conceivable human enterprise. It questions the approach made to reading, writing, running, keeping healthy, teaching, struggling, parenting, preaching and working. If you do not operate from an Africentric locus of control base, then you are in serious ethical and cultural trouble.

The foundations of Rites-Of-Passage beyond Africentricity are predicated on a minimum moral values system—Nguzo Saba (or Seven Principles) and rituals through ceremony. Minimum moral values or principles are important because without them, practice would be incorrect and possibilities would be limited. Principles are categories of commitment and priorities which define human possibilities and a value system. Such a value system is the Nguzo Saba or Seven Principles. The Nguzo Saba is based on Maulana Karenga's *Kawaida Theory* which maintains, "That if the key crisis in Black life is the cultural crisis, i.e., a crisis in views and values, then social organization or rather reorganization must start with a new value system."[4] The Nguzo Saba is the moral minimum value system African Americans need in order to rescue and reconstruct our history, humanity, and daily lives in our own image and interests. The seven principles are as follows:

Unity
To strive for and maintain unity in the family, community, ethnic group, nation, and planet.

Self-Determination
To define ourselves, name ourselves, create for ourselves, and speak for ourselves instead of being defined, named, created for, and spoken for by

70

others. Power is defining one's reality and having it accepted by others.

Collective Work and Responsibility
To build and maintain our community together and make our sister's and brother's problems our problems and to solve them together.

Cooperative Economics
To build and maintain our own stores, shops, and other businesses and to profit from them together.

Purpose
To make our collective vocation building and developing our community in order to restore our people to their traditional greatness.

Creativity
To do always as much as we can, in the way we can, in order to leave our community more beautiful and beneficial than we inherited it.

Faith
To believe with all our heart in ourselves, in our people, our parents, our teachers, a Creator, the righteousness and victory of our struggle.

Rituals through ceremony are important to internalize experiences. To become a rite or ritual, an activity need only be serious, established or prescribed by a legitimate authority, and formally performed at a designated time with appropriate symbolism. It is a ceremony and often a celebration of some kind. The following points are essential in implementing a ritualizing process:

71

- Give definite initial directions.
- Allow emotional expression and promote satisfaction at each step.
- Allow for consideration of other family members.
- Keep permanent records — snapshots, log, etc.
- Provide appropriate recognition for initiating or culminating age period, age, year or skill levels.
- Recognize an African extension from the past.
- Establish future behavior expectations.
- Make appropriate and accurate African custom references through research.

A ritual is the enactment of a myth. By participating in a ritual, you are participating in a myth. Myths are stories of our search through the ages for truth, for meaning, for significance. We all need to tell our story and understand our story. What happens when a society no longer embraces a powerful mythology? To find out what it means to have a society without any rituals, read your local and national newspapers. The news is full of destructive and violent acts by young people. We, as adults, have provided them no rituals by which they become members of the tribe or community.

Where do the youth growing in the community get their myths? They create their own. This is why we have graffiti. This is one of the significant reasons why gangs exist. Why do gangs have their own initiations and their own morality? In many instances, their laws are not those of the established institutions. They have not been initiated into the community.

RITES-OF-PASSAGE TRAINING MODELS

What is an example of a transformational model for youth that is predicated on the foundations of Rites-Of-Passage—centeredness, minimum moral standards, rituals, and ceremonies? In October, 1984, Simba Wachanga (Kiswahili for Young Lion), a transformational project was implemented at the East End Neighborhood House in Cleveland, Ohio. The project functioned as a guidance system through which Africa and America speak to their young males, telling them:

♦ Who they are!
♦ Where they should be going!
♦ What they need to do to get there!
♦ What they must have when they arrive!

In 1986, Simba Wachanga evolved into the Simba Wachanga Na Malaika Network. Malaika is Kiswahili for queen and was included as a womanhood developmental component. The addition of the womanhood development component was based on the premise that males and females are severed halves who by themselves are incomplete. Wholeness is a union of male and female. The network programming reflects separate gender tracks that intersect for special activities and occasions. In 1989, the Simba Na Malaika Network became the Ohio Rites-Of-Passage Network. The Network expanded services, developing a curriculum based on identified minimum standards and development/ implementation of an adult training process. Through such development and provision of training, the Network strives to maintain the integrity and quality of Rites-Of-Passage in the state of Ohio. The goals of

The Ohio Rites-Of-Passage Network are as follows:

Legitimization Of Being
Validation, worth, recognition, respect, and legitimacy.

Provision Of A Family Code
Guidelines for behaving in novel and/or confusing situations, aiding members in interpreting, managing, and responding to both known and undefined situations.

Elasticity Of Boundaries
Legitimization of being and provision of a family code produces an elasticity in African American interpersonal relationships. The unbreakable bond and associated rules of conduct give members the latitude and opportunity to stretch out and develop their own sense of "specialness" without fear of violating the brotherhood and familyhood. Members are provided opportunities to stretch out.

Provisions of Information/Knowledge
Provide members the benefit of shared insights and experiences, strengthening their ability to interpret and understand the events and happenings that affect their lives. The mutual sharing of knowledge and experience across generations heightens the individual member's ability to address, manage, and respond to the constantly changing conditions in their reality.

Mediation of Concrete Conditions
The ability to mediate conflicts and other conditions affecting its members provides strength and support. Interpersonal relations around problem

solving and decision making (in response to both external and internal issues), while constantly buffering and repairing the damage resulting from racism and oppression directed at its members is a critical strength.

Members will focus on the creation and maintenance of three (3) senses:

The Sense of History communicates to participants that we are, first and foremost, Africans. We are Africans because of our common cultural orientation which gives us the same sense of the natural universe and human condition that characterizes all African people.

The Sense of Community helps us understand that our identity and being is in the community. Community is our source of strength and not a burden to individual aspirations.

The Sense of Supreme Being helps us understand that there is power and a will that is greater than all else. The sense of the Supreme Being helps us realize that just as the natural path of living plants is to grow toward the sun, our natural path is to grow in understanding toward the Supreme Being.

The minimum standards or program objectives of The Ohio Rites-Of-Passage Network are:

◆ Develop an understanding of the Nguzo Saba or Seven Principles.

◆ Develop an understanding of African and African American History and Culture.

◆ Develop an understanding of the importance of well-being.

◆ Develop an understanding of spirituality.

◆ Develop an understanding of cooperative economic systems.

- Develop an understanding of self/environment as related to present/future.
- Develop an understanding of leadership.
- Develop an understanding of community services.
- Develop an understanding of government.
- Develop a fluency of basic Spanish and/or Kiswahili.
- Develop an understanding of manhood and womanhood.

The minimum standards or program objectives are predicated on the following prerequisites for male and female functioning:

Cognitive Domain:

Abilities to conceptualize, analyze, synthesize, infer, discriminate, and generalize.

Physical Domain:

Maximum development of physical well-being through education on: food and nutrition, exercise, sexuality, substance abuse, stress, and preventive disease living versus curative disease living.

Psychological/Emotional Domain:

Strong self-concept, trust, capacity for exploration and function, non-destructive defensive mechanisms and avoidance of mentally-destructive behaviors.

Affective Domain:

Exposure to the range of human emotions: anger, fear, love, warmth, sensitivity, caring, loss, hurt, pain, compassion, sharing, closeness, distance, support, encouragement, selfishness, emotional construction, and reconstruction.

Territorial Domain:
Self-defense and discipline.

Cultural Domain:
Black value system. African and African American culture. Family orientation, roles, responsibilities and accountability, work ethic and child rearing.

Spirituality:
Inseparability between the living and dead. Quietness and meditation with self and nature. Universal force. Living in harmony with, rather than in opposition to, the natural laws of universe, prayer, worship, and libation (acknowledgement and respect for ancestors).

The Ohio Rites-Of-Passage Network utilizes a course of studies which is composed of program and subject objectives. (Refer to Appendix for the course of studies). The course of studies can be modified and adjusted for age and maturity of participants. Programming by the Network has been neighborhood and schoolbased. Orientation and training of staff, trainers, volunteers (elders, mentors, parents, etc.), and interested parties/supporters is provided through a workshop or a series of weekend retreats.

Long-term training provided by The Ohio Rites-Of-Passage Network has been through Anthony Mensah, Ed.D. assisted by Reuben Harpole of Milwaukee, Wisconsin. Dr. Mensah, a Ghanian, is a respected elder, author, and master teacher who has been a scholar and practitioner of Rites-Of-Passage in the United States for over a generation. His model presents an intensive and comprehensive process that focuses on self-discovery, bonding, passages and rituals. The Mensah model sequence of topics per training are as follows:

♦ Rites-Of-Passage - definition
♦ The meaning of one's existence.
♦ Return to mother - the rediscovery of the ancestral past.
♦ The self - the rediscovery of your personal power.
♦ African philosophy of existence - nature's plan for all.
♦ The passages - life cycles.
♦ The territorial passages.
♦ Initiation rites in the African world.
♦ Initiation rites - the preparation.
♦ The initiation.
♦ Post-passage activities.

A complementary training model, which focuses on culturally-specific content for Rites-Of-Passage, has been developed through the leadership of Richard Kelsey, Ph.D., the author, and the Ohio Africentric Rites-Of-Passage Collective (1990). The four-phase content training model is as follows:

Basic Knowledge
    Historical overview
    Definitions
    Africentric Rites-Of-Passage
    Books and audio visuals
    Cultural exercises
    Values

Survival
  Physical fitness
  Nutrition
  Budgeting
  Wilderness training
  Career/life planning
  Values

Rituals
  Purpose
  Achievements
  Life events
  Names
  Values

Community Development
  Purpose
  Promotion
  Volunteers
  Institution support
  Values

Training as related to curriculum focuses on the following topics:

1. Accepting the goals of the curriculum.

2. Implementation of a balanced program of activities that strengthen the youths' skills in each of the areas of development (basic knowledge and history, survival, rituals, and community development).

3. Guidelines for selecting, designing, and implementing activities that encourages thinking skills.

4. Youths' learning processes.

5. The trainers and leaders role as a facilitator of learning-teaching methods.

The four-phase model is used to train youth service providers who have an interest in Rites-Of-Passage as a strategy for youth development. The Mensah and Kelsey models for training are complementary because one provides a framework or foundation for Rites-Of-Passage while the other provides the content for Rites-Of-Passage unique to the population. The content training focuses on two important issues within the four-phase model: the philosophical basis for the curriculum and the approach to learning.

For any Rites-Of-Passage Program, the development of a curriculum must reflect a historical reference point and cultural aesthetic; trainees must also understand curriculum is also influenced by the social, political, and spiritual perspectives desired for emphasis. The positions taken on these matters constitute the philosophical basis for curriculum. What is the historical reference point and where in time is it established? How will the movement of our people be treated, from the beginnings of human existence to the present? What is our relationship to Africa?

These questions determine how information will be presented within the structure of the program. These approaches constitute the foundation upon which information in the curriculum is organized and presented, as well as how individual participants perceive themselves and their own history.

What is your cultural aesthetic? By whose cultural standards do you measure yourself and your accomplishments? For example, what is success? Does it mean that you are successful if you are the first African American to be recognized for doing what other Americans have done throughout history? Do you grasp the forefront of a movement and make a contribution that no one else has made? Must you be original in solving problems facing your own communities? Should you encourage participants to take the skills you have worked so hard to develop in them and apply them outside our community? Your cultural aesthetic will help you find a reference point, but it also helps you decide what you mean by concepts such as human worth, beauty, appreciation for the arts, and other things you value. How will the curriculum content reflect these issues of aesthetics? Wade Nobles has pointed out that the task of the family, parents, teachers and concerned adults is to prepare our children to live and be among White people without becoming White people.[5]

What is your social and political perspective on the proper relationships among and between groups in society and issues of empowerment? For example, how will the curriculum address specific issues like the secession movement of Roxbury (Boston) from the United States in 1986 and apartheid in South Africa? Will the curriculum prepare students to interpret future issues from an African American perspective? What is your spiritual perspective? What role will religion have in the curriculum and what values are to be stressed? Where will you place the focus of your curriculum on the continuum, between a spiritual or a materialistic interpretation?

Why focus on Africa as a reference point for the treatment of history, culture, politics, and spirituality in the curriculum? It is not to recreate Africa here in the United States. It is to internalize the concept of Africa as part of our perspective and to point out the contributions of Africa and Africans to our development. It is also done to recognize that cultural and academic excellence are of equal importance; youth cannot achieve academic excellence and yet know nothing about their culture. Furthermore, the social knowledge we obtain from other people determines the priorities we establish in applying scientific knowledge. If we are going to learn about computers in our curriculum, what will we as African Americans do with the computers in our lives? It is important for Rites-Of-Passage content specialists to understand that youth interpret their experiences and their environment differently and use different forms of logic to arrive at their various points of view. The staff can be most effective when they are flexible, adapting their instruction to multiple learning styles, because not all learning occurs in a one-way movement from adult volunteer to participant.

There are two methods of instruction content specialists should use. One is the instructor-directed approach and the other is participant-directed approach. In the instructor-directed approach, most of the decisions about what will be discussed are made by the content specialist. The focus also is on products of learning, which often leads to rote responses. Youth tend to give you what you ask for, but they have not internalized how to arrive at a particular point of view. They will recite pledges without knowing the meaning of the pledge. With this type of learning, instructors may feel that they have accomplished something when, in fact, they have not. The participant-directed approach focuses on discovery, allowing instructors to build learning experiences around students exploring for themselves. Here, the emphasis is on process or how information is learned. Participants are involved in field trips, interviews, bringing people to the skill activity, and so forth. Instructors may not see immediate results, but learning is taking place.

An understanding of culture and cognition is vital to the success of designing curriculum that matches the learning styles of African American children. Janice Hale Benson[6] and Jawanza Kunjufu[7] identify learning styles and relevant curriculum for developing positive self-images and discipline in African American children. Youth learn ninety percent of what they do, fifty percent of what they see, and only ten percent of what they hear. "Learning by doing", utilizing a circular learning approach rather than a linear approach, is African in nature and approximates the learning styles of African American youth.

Life is a succession of stages or passages. We are not unlike the lobster. The lobster grows by developing and shedding a series of hard, protective shells. Each time it expands from within, the confining shell must be sloughed off. It is left exposed and vulnerable until, in time, a new covering grows to replace the old. With each passage from one stage growth to the next, we too, must shed a protective structure. We are left exposed and vulnerable—but also lively and embryonic again, capable of growing in ways we hadn't known before. Everything that happens to us: birthdays, baptism, graduations, getting a job, losing a job, marriage, childbirth, divorce, and death affects us.

The experiences of existing adolescent rites, societies, and projects reflect three stages: pre-passage, passage, and the passage ceremony. Pre-passage involves fulfilling the specified age-group requirements. Passage is a period of demonstration and practical application of acquired competencies and skills. Passage is the bridging or transformation period. It is a prelude to a metamorphosis, to young manhood. When passage is final, a boy dies and a young man is born. The death of the child and his reincarnation as a man is the final bridge that must be crossed to enter adulthood as a young man. The distinction or honor of becoming an initiate or wearing the regalia of an initiate must be earned and sanctioned through the passage ceremony.

The length of time of Rites-Of-Passage societies and programs vary from a lifetime to a minimum of one year. The Ohio Rites-Of-Passage Network pre-passage period is seven months and five months for the passage period. The passage period requires demonstration in the following achievement areas (a composite of the minimum standards or basic skill areas—history, culture and life skills):

♦ Communication and organizational skills
♦ Maintaining a written log/scrapbook
♦ Autobiography
♦ Biography (male and female)
♦ Speeches
♦ Solitude and ordeal with self and nature
♦ Wilderness survival
♦ Retrieval and organization of information
♦ Family Tree, interview of elders
♦ Decision making and problem solving

+ Fund raising, career exploration/planning
+ Special life skills include: meal preparation for group, garden maintenance, health project, arts and craft project, written examination (Nguzo Saba, Kwanzaa symbols, history, etc.), maintaining good grades and positive attitude in school, family and community

Rites-Of-Passage ceremonies reflect the following general format:

+ Welcoming
+ Libation (honoring the ancestors)
+ Audience participation (call and response, litany of the people)
+ Testimony
+ Challenge by relatives and friends
+ Recognition by significant others
+ Music/dance/poetry
+ Prepared speech by initiate
+ Feast
+ Passage ceremony symbols and artifacts include but are not limited to the following: Seven candles in holder (three red, one black, three green)
+ Unity cup filled with water for libation
+ Bowl with earth
+ Straw mat
+ Nation flag (red, black, green)
+ Cornstalk (to be burned, symbolizing death of the boy)

- Medallion (engraved with continent of Africa, outline of U.S.A. inside Africa, color scheme of red, black, green)
- Banner (incorporating Seven Principles)

In conclusion, Rites-Of-Passage, be it family, religious, school, or community-based, must be Africentric and grounded in the Black value system. A thorough understanding and operation of such a process and its values are crucial. Rites-Of-Passage is part of an African tradition that must be reinstitutionalized. The Rites-Of-Passage concept provides an opportunity to nurture and develop a much needed generation of African American men.

The road ahead will not be easy; the greatest challenge is institutionalization of Rites-Of-Passage as a way of life through community socialization.

In his poem "To Smile on Autumn", photojournalist Gordon Parks recalls his father's advice on life. If a man can reach the latter days of life with his soul intact, he has mastered life. For Black men who survive into their sixties and beyond, reaching the spiritual heights Parks speaks of is a sweet finale. We as men and women, hopefully, can approach this finale having left our children a legacy. "I want all my children and your children to be proud of me. I want them to say, I provided them, not only with material things, but with care. I want them to say 'my parents and community gave me a vision of myself, and a foundation to build on'."

The time has come for men in the African American community to stand up and be counted. All we have to lose are our children and future.

Without an Africentric orientation, our youth are susceptible to extrinsic values.

87

Africentricity has produced some of the . . .

richest and most beautiful elements of culture.

CHAPTER FOUR

Africentricity: A New Way Of Life

Bobby E.
Wright, Ph.D.

*Blacks have charismatic leaders
and others have institutions.*

When Dr. Martin Luther King, Jr. was buried on April 9, 1968, SCLC was buried with him. However, Kennedy is assassinated; Johnson refuses to run for a second term; Nixon resigns before impeachment; Ford is replaced by a Southern plantation owner; a movie star's time runs out and yet, with all these changes in heads of state, in spite of all those changes, there was consistent behavior by all of them on almost every issue, e.g., the treatment of African Americans as a group. It must be understood that institutions have very little to do with buildings or anything concrete, rather they are methods and ideas which sustain a social theory or in the vernacular, "continue a way of life."

The Portuguese, Dutch, English, French, etc., leave Africa, but their institutions remain which perpetuate their values, language, behaviors and belief system. In fact, Africans worldwide continue to be trained by these institutions rather than educated–training is defined as being manipulated to bring into the desired form of the oppressor. Education is defined as acquiring knowledge and developing the powers of reasoning in order to develop and sustain one's own people and culture.

The process of African Americans creating our own reality and taking control of the socialization of our youth involves Rites-Of-Passage that is African-centered. To avoid the possibility of confusion, it is important to point out that Rites-Of-Passage is not separate from the socialization continuum. Rather such rites should be regarded as areas of reinforcement and elevated affirmation in the socialization process. Author and youth advocate, Useni Perkins of Chicago has incorporated Anthony Mensah's Rites-Of-Passage Matrices to develop an Africentric Socialization Paradigm for the positive development of Black people (see page 120). The paradigm or model presents a way of thinking and doing that is not "new" but "old". Rites-Of-Passage is subsumed within the Perkins conceptual model and is a means for acculturation within the socialization process. The major objectives as defined by Useni Perkins for Africentric Rites-Of-Passage are as follows:

♦ to help a youth achieve a sense of his/her true identity and a feeling of belonging and commitment to the Black community and diaspora.

♦ to help a youth achieve a level of social maturity and awareness that will enable him/her to function in a racist society without engaging in self-defeating behavior.

♦ to help a youth realize and achieve masculine and/or feminine roles that are satisfying, responsible, and consistent with acceptable cultural norms and values.

♦ to help a youth develop a philosophy of life which allows him/her to function in a responsible and mature manner.

♦ to help a youth to relate positively to his/her parents, peers, extended family, teachers, and elders.

The advent of Rites-Of-Passage and Africentricity are Western concepts that do not translate in any West African language. Both exist as a way of life. The nearest equivalent to Rites-Of-Passage in Africa is the traditional African educational system. Rites-Of-Passage, as a part of the Africentric socialization model, is a confirmation/affirmation that recognizes who we are during our quest for identity at the various stages of life.

Rites-Of-Passage within the preceding chapters was presented as a strategy for the coming of age of the African American male. However, Rites-Of-Passage is not for everyone and should not be regarded as a panacea. Rites-Of-Passage should not be presented as a quick-fix solution. Rites-Of-Passage in an ideal environment requires maintenance of codes, performing established rituals, reaffirming familial/community obligations, stability, and homogeneity. In many instances, what is being

91

presented as Rites-Of-Passage is nothing more than big brother, mentoring, self-esteem, and manhood development programs. Rites-Of-Passage is the union of all these components and more. Intent is judged by answering the question: Is it in the best interest of the community? The Nguzo Saba or Seven Principles should be used as a criteria in answering the question.

RITES-OF-PASSAGE AS AN INSTITUTION

What should be expected in the efforts to institutionalize Africentric Rites-Of-Passage through community socialization? The study and practice of Rites-Of-Passage and Africentricity have been resisted because of fear of anything associated with Africa! Africentric Rites-Of-Passage is resisted by many Black religious leaders because it is perceived as a competing belief system that is rooted in worshiping "dead bones" through libation and is labeled too "African".

The existing values and world view of Western society are contrary to the needs of African Americans. Any movements of self-determination in the African American community to redefine our reality or strategies to reaffirm and confirm our peoplehood in methods other than mainstream cultural context are resisted. It is also argued, "despite the growing rhetoric of acceptance of ethnicity and strong ethnic identification in the larger American society, educators and school officials continue to disapprove of a strong ethnic identity among Black adolescents. These contradictory messages produce conflict and ambivalence in adolescents, both

92

toward developing strong racial and ethnic identities and toward performing well in school."[1]

On the other hand, within the African American community, many of us are narrowly interpreting and practicing Africentricity and Rites-Of-Passage. A lack of tolerance for differences and other ideas is becoming the rule and not the exception in circles of discussion. Issues such as the following are being debated: Who is more Africentric? Who is more Black? Who is more knowledgeable of Nile Valley civilization and can read hieroglyphics? Should biracial youth be accepted in Africentric Rites-Of-Passage programs? Should children of non-African ancestry be accepted in publicly-funded Africentric Rites-Of-Passage programs? Such issues reflect an internalization of the bitterness and pain of our American holocaust. The burden of White male supremacy and maleness in a macho sense has immobilized too many African American males. We are in a constant state of reaction and being held hostage by our egos.

However, history is finally on our side; our challenge as a people is to get on the right side of history.

The social theory of Africentricity and the process of Rites-Of-Passage provide us with the potential for practicing a way of life that is the only way, to the primordial center of our being. Rites-Of-Passage through Africentric socialization is another chance, another way; it is the harbinger, as W.E.B. DuBois said, "of that bright tomorrow which is yet destined to soften the harshness of the teutonic today."

It's hard to tell time by revolutionary clocks. Everything including time, changes in a revolutionary time and the clocks inherited from the old regime are usually too slow or too fast.

93

A real revolution introduces a new time, a new space, and a new relation to both time and space. Within that shifting space-time continuum, men who stand still find that they no longer occupy the same coordinates in relation to a moving reality.

Africentricity and Rites-Of-Passage offer Africans-in-America a chance to find or lose our way. We have a mandate from history, a mandate from the living, the dead, and the unborn, to make this moment count by using the time and resources history has given. This is a serious responsibility; what we do now and what we fail to do will determine the destiny of the world. We are moving toward a point of no return in America and Rites-Of-Passage through Africentric socialization provides us with an opportunity and experience to ask ourselves the following:

Question
Who am I?

Criterion
What values, history, traditions and cultural precepts do I recognize, respect, and practice?

Question
Am I really who I think I am?

Criterion
To what extent do I have to understand, internalize, employ, and reflect the cultural authenticity of my people?

Question
Am I all I ought to be?

Criterion

To what extent do I possess and consciously apply the enduring cultural standards and meanings which measure the "being" and "becoming" of Black people in terms of our cultural substance and concrete conditions?

We cannot afford to continue being blinded by the "isms" of our American experiences and paralyzed by our egos. The results have been divisive and disastrous. A Eurocentric or segmented world view is the dominant conceptual system of socialization in this society. Africentricity must be interpreted as an optimal or holistic conceptual system that functions to maximize positivity and the greatest good (Refer to page 118 for Conceptual Analysis by Linda Meyers, Ph.D.).

Africentricity reaffirms the creative wisdom of the ancient and the modern, emphasizing the unifying principles underlying each perspective, providing the ground, a centering. The world view of Africentricity is by no means exclusionary. From this reality, it is not surprising that the same basic, ancient wisdom has been found throughout the world. The seeds of this ancient knowledge can prove to be the salvation of science and practice in our modern world.

In charting the course for institutionalizing Rites-Of-Passage through Africentric socialization three areas need to be clarified—success, social identity, and mid-life passage.

The barometer of success within the past was based on individual effort, merit and accomplishment. Success, as related to an Africentric socialization process, means Blacks must succeed as a people, not just as individuals. Rites-Of-Passage must be a group phenomenon based on success of the group or age-set. The operative is "win-win", not "win-lose". The basic premise of African philosophy of existence was: "Every person has a built-in capacity to succeed."

A SPIRITUAL KINSHIP

In studying the social identity and cultural frame of reference among Africans-in-America, the concept kinship of spirit has proven to be useful. It suggests a kinship-like connection between and among persons in a society, not related by blood or marriage, who have maintained essential reciprocal spiritual, social, economic, and political functions. The term conveys the idea of "brotherhood" and "sisterhood" of all Black Americans — a sense of peoplehood or collective social identity.

The term kinship of spirit denotes a cultural symbol of collective identity and is based on more than just skin color. The term also implies the particular mindset or world view of those persons who are considered to be group members and is used to denote the moral judgment the group makes on its members. Essentially, the concept suggests that merely possessing African features or being of African descent does not automatically make one a member in good standing of the group. One can be denied membership by the group because his/her behavior, attitudes, and activities are perceived as being at odds with those thought to be appropriate. Only Blacks are involved in the evaluation of group members' eligible for membership in this kinship system; thus, we control the criteria used to judge one's worthiness for membership. That is, the determination of the criteria for membership in the kinship of spirit system rests solely within the Black community. Furthermore, criteria for kinship of spirit has a special significance for Black people, because they are regarded as the ideal by which members of the group are judged. This judgment is also the medium through which Black America distinguishes "real" from "spurious" members of the community. An example of a kinship of spirit system in the Americas would be the institutionalization and practice of Candomble among Bahians in Brazil.

The process of "Africanization" has produced some of the richest and most beautiful elements of culture. They are indeed testaments to the strength and resilience of African culture, often even amazing Africans who have recently come from the Motherland. What a shame that many of those who take these traditions for granted do not know that they are African.

The Candomble in Bahia, Brazil is perhaps the greatest achievement of primal African tradition in the diaspora. Through disciplined adherence to African principles of education, religious hierarchy, and ritual, African descendants in Bahia have re-created and maintained their religious traditions. These traditions compare with and, in some cases, even surpass traditional religious organization in Nigeria (its place of origin), where European influences have affected traditional patterns.

The Candomble is based in Yoruba, Ewe, Congo and Fon traditions. Its members have maintained contact with Africa by sea and maritime trade through which they obtained authentic articles needed for the practice of their religion. The backbone of African religious organization is the process of initiation, training, and ritual through which novices gain knowledge of the spirits and of ritual practice. The priests and priestesses, brought forcibly from Africa, came determined to keep their traditions intact in the belief that the greatest protection their people had was their intense and close relationship with the spirit world. The discipline and precision of the religious structure and training process was to make this African-Bahian Candomble the most respected manifestation of the African religion tradition in new Europe.

The centers where Candomble is practiced are called Terreiros. It is estimated in the city of Salvador (1.5 million), there are at least two thousand Terreiros. This number testifies to the vitality of the religion. Candomble is practiced as a way-of-life in a kinship of spirit setting. The Terreiro is headed by a priestess and serves not only a spiritual but social function. It is an excellent example of Africentric socialization that utilizes rituals and ceremonies. The emphasis on developing political and nationalist consciousness is lacking because the country has only recently come from under the oppression/repression of a military dictatorship and police state. However, some Terreiros are incorporating political and nationalistic consciousness development as part of their socialization process.

Another example of an institutionalized kinship of spirit system that is African-centered is the Bahian Samba schools.

After the abolition of Brazilian slavery in 1888, the African rituals sprang back; they became Brazilianized under the names Samba and Candomble and their power was undiminished.

Carnival, as an African-rooted institution, is expressed through Samba schools whose membership incorporate entire communities of poor and oppressed Bahians. The Samba schools are social, political, and economic institutions that transport the Sambistra during Carnival into a "dream time" that is the real world where lives move forward rather than repetitively around themselves, where things look the way they're supposed to and actions have consequences.

In 1988, the Samba school, Mangueira won first place. A stanza from their theme song was as follows:

The Black race came to this country,

Bringing their strong arms and their roots.

They planted their culture here,

Yoruba, Gege and Nago.

In the refineries, mines and fields,

Blacks were always oppressed,

And in the rebel enclave of Palmares

Zumbi our leader fought for freedom.

Carnival and Candomble represent a corpus of philosophy, attitudes, preferences, values, beliefs and behavior—all of which have been transmitted through Africentric space and woven with a strong spirituality. The lack of cultural continuity among North American Blacks because of weak African retention has limited the institutionalization of anything comparable to Carnival or Candomble.

The closest equivalent to Carnival or Candomble in the United States would be the African American celebration, Kwanzaa. Kwanzaa, as originated by

Maulana Karenga, provides the portal to an Afri-centric world. Rites-Of-Passage, as generally prac-ticed in the United States, is a pragmatic extension of the principles of Kwanzaa. Rites-Of-Passage, as practiced by the Ohio Rites-Of-Passage Network, is an outgrowth of the countywide organizing and celebrations of Kwanzaa by the East End Neighbor-hood House of Cleveland, Ohio.

Most Rites-Of-Passage efforts in our communities reflect an incorporation of the Nguzo Saba or seven principles of Kwanzaa. The institutionalization of Kwanzaa is evidenced by its increasing appeal and participation by the masses throughout the United States. Kwanzaa reinforces Africentric values and principles (unity, self determination, collective work and responsibility, cooperative economics, purpose, creativity and faith); to many participants of the celebration, the principles have become a prescrip-tion for living.

Some communities and organizations such as the Ohio Rites-Of-Passage Network have Rites-Of-Pas-sage induction, transition, or naming ceremonies at the time of Kwanzaa when generally the maximum number of African Americans will be present. An evolving institution, Kwanzaa has been the impetus for the initial resurgence of Rites-Of-Passage in the African American community.

OVERCOMING LIFE CRISES

Anthropologist Arnold Van Gennep's book, *The Rites-Of-Passage*, was first published in 1908. His work provides a widely-used framework for the dis-cussion of Rites-Of-Passage in any culture. Van Gennep defined "life crises" as those crucial mo-ments when we pass from one state of being to the next. Puberty or adolescence is one of those crucial moments.

If becoming a man means crossing the river of childhood to enter the land of maturity, adolescence can be thought of as the search for the proper vessel to set sail in and complete the journey. The "proper vessel" that was once supplied by formalized Rites-Of-Passage has been lost. The results have been described in the book Isaiah, Chapter 3, "The Lord will let the people be governed by immature boys. Everyone will take advantage of everyone else. Young people will not respect their elders...". However, Proverbs 22:6 states, "Train up a child in the way he would go and when he is old he will not depart from it."

The lack of initiation through Rites-Of-Passage during adolescence is a major contributor to male irresponsibility and modern "mid-life crisis." And so today, mid-life crisis ranks as one of our most important times of transition. We face this passage without aid of historically-sanctioned traditions or precedents from previous cultures. Many of us too, must face this passage without the benefit of a successful completion of a prior initiation. Such an initiation would have provided a male with the strength and feeling of self-worth that would serve him well in overcoming the personal anxieties he might encounter with respect to the aging process. Furthermore, initiated males in the past enjoyed considerable authority and prestige, upon reaching middle age.

However, if our manhood was never fully affirmed during youth, this time of transition presents even greater dangers to our personal sense of well-being. And the passage is made even more difficult by the absence of any social structures to help us through. Just as the modern transition from boyhood into manhood is made alone with private symbols, the mid-life passage must be accomplished the same way. Yet mid-life passage is certainly in keeping with contemporary idioms. Just as each individual man must face up to the loss of his strength during the mid-life transition, so too must modern-day men collectively face up to the decline of physical strength as a defining characteristic of manhood.

Among the Nomadic Masai of Eastern Africa, the mid-life age period is called Ilpayiani. During this period former senior warriors understand, "now that you are a junior elder drop your weapons and use your head and wisdom—master the art of the tongue and wisdom of mind."[2] The classical image of man as a hunter and warrior—an image best realized in adulthood—must now be transcended. Such a transition not only faces modern-day men collectively, but our society as a whole which is facing its mid-life crisis.

The modern mid-life crisis points to a further fragmentation of the initiation process. The temporal fragmentation of the initiation process is played out in many ways. Divorce can be as important to the developmental process of maturation as a man's early sexual encounters. The decline of our athletic prowess at the onset of middle age presents at least as much of a personal challenge as do the athletic events in which we participate during the prime of our youth. Facing up to a limited career and job presents as true a test of manhood as does the preparation for work and work experience undertaken by the fortunate few of us at an earlier age. And even in war, the readjustment of civilian life can be as trying as the experience of battle; twenty some years after the war has ended, many Vietnam veterans are still struggling with their re-entry into American life. This second round of tasks are as important to the realization of manhood as the earlier challenges and yet these new tasks are not often encountered, let alone overcome, until men are well past the age of their first and more traditional initiations.

The whole question of age raises other issues relating to our contemporary images of manhood. Today, we do not generally emulate our elders or hold them in high esteem. We see age as an adversary rather than an ally in the developmental process, a regrettable reality which is to be avoided if possible, or at least suppressed. "The primacy of youth within our culture serves as a significant impediment to any simulation of a classical process of initiation, for without tribal elders who are universally respected and revered, an initiation is likely to suffer from a loss of viable authority—and since the initiation is not appropriately sanctioned, it is unlikely to have as meaningful and complete an impact upon the participating individuals."[3]

The modern and Western image of manhood, colored as it is by our collective phobia of the natural aging process, becomes unduly restricted. We implicitly think of "manhood" as equivalent to young manhood, roughly between the ages of twenty and forty. After that, we tend to think that manhood begins a gradual decline, as if the onset of hemorrhoids, the loss of hair, and a weakening of body tissues somehow manage to negate the manly virtues and reverse the maturation process. This is indeed ironic, for the physical strength of youth, which we now equate with manhood, is no longer objectively necessary for our social and economic functioning.

In May, 1991, the Ohio Rites-Of-Passage Network began providing a series of adult Rites-Of-Passage retreats with an initiation. Such an experience is needed to fill a void in the life of many uninitiated adults. As noted by Nsenga Warfield-Coppock, there are groups mostly well-entrenched in African American communities which have comprehensive life cycle Rites-Of-Passage. "The groups form a foundation for the regulation and oversight of the members within their purview."[4] Often these groups establish a structure that will address the holistic developmental needs of the community. Some of these groups have established regular acknowledgements of the rites by age groups. Some establish guidelines for approximated changes in life cycle development and others suggest that every 7 years there should be an acknowledgement of celebration. At birth, the naming ceremony is performed. At ages 13-15, the puberty rite is performed. At age 28, the adulthood entry is made. Junior eldership is performed at 45 with senior eldership status and honor recognized at 62 years.

Where does Rites-Of-Passage go from here? First, Rites-Of-Passage exists as a strategy for life cycle development and not a panacea for resurrection of the masses. Aside from life cycle development, Rites-Of-Passage can focus on substance abuse rehabilitation, teen pregnancy or teen fathers, high risk or primary prevention and self development or therapeutic milieu. Rites-Of-Passage can also be used to augment existing programs. Programs can remain intact but can be augmented with the cultural or other aspects of Rites-Of-Passage. The Boy Scouts could incorporate a Rites-Of-Passage merit badge for Black troops.

The use of Rites-Of-Passage and initiation as a social prescription is valid. However, using rites and initiation only as a prescription for social ills compromise their intent as a means for community socialization. Rites and initiation are subsumed within the socialization process. Rites and initiation do not come after the fact; they create the fact. Through an Africentric socialization model incorporating a Rites-Of-Passage Matrices, we strive to create an African instinct that regulates behaviors.

Institutionalizing such a model continues to be a challenge. Established institutions within the community such as churches and mosques have resisted the model because it is perceived as a competitor that is contrary to their belief system. However, visionary and responsive leadership through Reverends Frank Fair, Chester, Pennsylvania, Willie Wilson, Washington, D.C. Wendell Anthony, Detroit, Michigan, Michael Exum and Mark Olds, Cleveland, Pastor Jeremiah Wright, Chicago, and Bishop George Stallings, Washington D.C., and Los Angeles, and others are institutionalizing Christocentric Rites-Of-Passage.

Another challenge to institutionalizing Rites-Of-Passage relates to the first passage phase of separation. Traditional Rites-Of-Passage and initiation involved separation that was physical from familiar surroundings. Physical separation was enough to begin the process. However, modern Rites-Of-Passage necessitates much more than physical separation. A weekend retreat in the natural surroundings of the country does not ensure the psychological separation from our habitual Eurocentric thinking process. Many that are proclaiming to be Africentric continue to use Eurocentric thought processes. The filter is Africentric but the base continues to be Eurocentric.

Psychological separation from Eurocentric thinking is not a short-term task. It will require long-term training under those few among us who have incorporated our own particular existence within a greater reality. Such individuals walk in dream time or the two realities described by the Aborigines of Australia — dreams are the shadows of reality. Such an individual is represented by Elder Anthony Mensah, a native Ghanian now residing in Milwaukee, who along with his mentee Reuben Harpole of Milwaukee provide Rites-Of-Passage training. Coming of age for the African American male through Africentric Rites-Of-Passage is limited only by the creativity of those wishing to re-establish the way. What has been presented is something old that has been rediscovered, something that has been returned to us through the great ancestor with the following message:

Power must be handled in the manner of holding an egg in the hand: If you hold it too firmly it breaks; if you hold it too loosely it drops.

APPENDIX

COURSE OF STUDY
PROGRAM/SUBJECT OBJECTIVES
PROGRAM OBJECTIVE

1. Initiates will understand the Nguzo Saba (Seven Principles) minimum value system.

SUBJECT OBJECTIVES
Initiates will:

1.1 define the Nguzo Saba

1.2 memorize and recite the Seven Principles in Kiswahili and English

1.3 write the Seven Principles in Kiswahili and in English

1.4 discuss the meaning of the Seven Principles

1.5 define values

1.6   discuss the origin of the African American Flag (Bendera)

1.7   understand the symbolism of the African American Flag

1.8   participate in a Kwanzaa ritual

1.9   become familiar with basic Kiswahili terms

1.10 memorize and recite project pledge

1.11 memorize and recite the Black National Anthem (Lift Every Voice)

1.12 demonstrate an incorporation of the Nguzo Saba Principles in their daily lives

COURSE OF STUDY
PROGRAM/SUBJECT OBJECTIVES
PROGRAM OBJECTIVE

2.   Initiates will develop an understanding of African and African American History and culture.

SUBJECT OBJECTIVE
Initiates will:

2.1   define his-tory and my-story

2.2   understand the differences between African and African American History

2.3   identify the birthplace of the original man and woman

2.4   draw a map of Africa and identify all nations and capitals

108

2.5 identify the great African civilizations (Ethiopia, Nile Valley, Egypt, Ghana, Mali, Songhay, Kenya, Zimbabwe, Azania)

2.6 understand the contributions of Africa to Western civilization and World History

2.7 discuss the pyramids and Egyptian alphabet (Hieroglyphics)

2.8 design a pyramid

2.9 discuss the Olmec civilization and pre-Columbian contact

2.10 discuss the many invaders of Africa (Asians, Arabs, Greeks, Romans and Northern Europeans)

2.11 explain why Africans allowed invaders to settle along the coast

2.12 discuss the underdevelopment of Africa by Europe

2.13 understand the differences in slavery as practiced by Africans, Arabs, and Europeans

2.14 demonstrate an appreciation for the ancestors who survived during the Middle Passage

2.15 discuss Africa's resistance to slavery (North America, South America, Brazil, Haiti, etc.)

2.16 discuss interaction between enslaved Africans and ancestors in America with indigenous populations (Creek, Cherokees, Seminoles, etc.)

2.17 discuss the uniqueness of New Orleans and South Sea Islands (South Carolina and Georgia), as related to African American history and culture

COURSE OF STUDY
PROGRAM/SUBJECT OBJECTIVES
PROGRAM OBJECTIVE

3. Initiates will understand the importance of wellness.

SUBJECT OBJECTIVES
Initiates will:

3.1 demonstrate basic self-defense

3.2 understand the importance of proper nutrition

3.3 prepare a well-rounded meal

3.4 demonstrate ability to survive in a natural environment with basic supplies and equipment

3.5 demonstrate a knowledge of basic first aid and CPR

3.6 demonstrate basic swimming ability

3.7 demonstrate physical fitness ability

3.8 understand the importance of health and personal hygiene

3.9 define human sexuality—sexual responsibility and sexual liability, i.e. AIDS, STDS, pregnancy

COURSE OF STUDY
PROGRAM/SUBJECT OBJECTIVES
PROGRAM OBJECTIVE

4. Initiates will understand the importance of spirituality.

SUBJECT OBJECTIVES
Initiates will:

4.1 discuss spirituality

4.2 distinguish between "religion" and "spirituality"

4.3 discuss the role spirituality has played in the lives of Africans of the Diaspora

4.4 discuss Creation stories

4.5 identify the Pharaoh Akhenaten (Amen-hotep)

4.6 discuss African traditional religion

4.7 discuss the significance of traditional African rituals and libation

4.8 discuss how Africans were denied the worship of their traditional religion

4.9 discuss the Egyptian 42 Negative Confessions and its relationship to the Ten Commandments

4.10 discuss the African contribution to religion

COURSE OF STUDY
PROGRAM/SUBJECT OBJECTIVES
PROGRAM OBJECTIVE

5. Initiates will develop an understanding of Cooperative Economic Systems.

SUBJECT OBJECTIVES
The initiates will:

5.1 define economics

5.2 discuss scarcity

5.3 explain natural resources

5.4 differentiate between "wants" and "needs"

5.5 discuss "competition" and "cooperation"

5.6 discuss marketing, media, and subliminal seduction

5.7 differentiate between idealism and realism

5.8 understand a system and institution

5.9 compare various economic systems

5.10 explain economic problems facing the African American community (differentiate between consumers and producers)

5.11 understand and develop a business plan

5.12 understand the interrelationship between the Western Economy and the World Economy

COURSE OF STUDY
PROGRAM/SUBJECT OBJECTIVES
PROGRAM OBJECTIVE

6.   Initiates will develop decision-making skills for self-awareness and personal planning.

SUBJECT OBJECTIVES
Initiates will:

6.1   identify one's life as related to present and future visions

6.2   discuss attitudes and how they affect your future

6.3   recognize personal values

6.4   establish goals and objectives

6.5   differentiate between a job and career

6.6   develop a career plan

COURSE OF STUDY
PROGRAM/SUBJECT OBJECTIVES
PROGRAM OBJECTIVE

7.   Initiates will understand the importance of leadership.

SUBJECT OBJECTIVES
Initiates will:

7.1   identify the qualities of leadership

7.2   understand how leadership is developed

7.3   understand the responsibilities of leadership

7.4   understand the differences between a leader and a follower

7.5   identify and understand conflict and cooperation

7.6   identify and understand resolutions to conflict

7.7   identify and discuss historical and contemporary leaders

7.8   develop speaking skills

7.9   develop an agenda and chair a meeting

7.10 research, study and debate opposing viewpoints and interpretation of current local, national, and international issues

COURSE OF STUDY
PROGRAM/SUBJECT OBJECTIVES
PROGRAM OBJECTIVE

8.   Initiates will understand the concept of community services.

SUBJECT OBJECTIVES
Initiates will:

8.1   define community

8.2   define the relationship between self/family/community

8.3   identify modes of community involvement

8.4   understand civic responsibility and volunteerism

8.5   understand the difference between

organizing and providing services to
address community needs and issues

8.6 discuss how to organize for change

8.7 define issues and program for change
(program, unity, alliances, action)

8.8 develop a position paper including
problem identification, analysis and
resolution, (draft, feedback, edit, and
final adoption)

8.9 complete 30 hours of community services

COURSE OF STUDY
PROGRAM/SUBJECT OBJECTIVES
PROGRAM OBJECTIVE

9. Initiates will develop an understanding of
government.

SUBJECT OBJECTIVES
Initiates will:

9.1 discuss and understand purposes and
need for government

9.2 discuss the concept of power

9.3 define centralized and decentralized
power

9.4 understand various forms of government

9.5 explain the concept of "survival of the
Tribe"

9.6 demonstrate an understanding of
"community"

9.7   discuss the six nation confederation and its relation to the U.S. Constitution

9.8   discuss constitutional law

9.9   review African traditional, constitutional and customary laws

9.10 demonstrate an understanding of "interest groups"

9.11 demonstrate a basic understanding of the origin, ideas, realities, and contradictions of the American Constitution

9.12 understand a two-party system

9.13 discuss independent party politics

9.14 discuss African American political leadership

COURSE OF STUDY
PROGRAM/SUBJECT OBJECTIVES
PROGRAM OBJECTIVE

10.   Initiates will develop an understanding and basic fluency in Spanish and/or Kiswahili/ Twi.

SUBJECT OBJECTIVES
Initiates will:

10.1 learn the sounds and pronunciation

10.2 learn basic expressions

10.3 learn to count

10.4 learn the colors

10.5 learn the days of the week/greetings

10.6 learn to tell time

10.7 learn basic grammar

COURSE OF STUDY
PROGRAM/SUBJECT OBJECTIVES
PROGRAM OBJECTIVE

11. Initiates will develop an understanding of manhood and womanhood.

SUBJECT OBJECTIVES
Initiates will:

11.1 differentiate between males and men, females and women

11.2 discuss male and female stereotypes

11.3 discuss the hazards of assuming male and female stereotypical roles

11.4 identify different ways in which males and females suppress emotion

11.5 compare and contrast how males and females show or avoid showing emotions

11.6 discuss the consequences of suppressing emotion

11.7 identify the male code of conduct

11.8 identify some of the consequences of acting tough

11.9 define a man and woman

Conceptual Systems
(Linda Meyers, Ph.D.)

Assumption	Optimal	Sub-Optimal
Ontology (nature of reality)	Spiritual (Known in an extra-sensory fashion) and material (known through the five senses) as one	Material with possible spiritual aspect that is separate and secondary
Epistemology (nature of Knowledge)	Self-knowledge known through symbolic imagery and rhythm	External knowledge known through counting and measuring
Axiology (nature of value)	Highest value in positive inter-personal relationship among persons	Highest value in objects or acquisitions of objects
Logic (reason)	Diunital--union of opposites (both/and)	Dichotomous--dividing into two (either/or)
Process	Ntuology--all sets are inter-related through human and spiritual networks	Technology-- all sets are repeatable and reproducible
Identity/Self worth	Multi-dimensional self-intrinsic in being	Individual form based on external criteria or materialism
Values guiding behavior	Spiritualism, openess w/nature, communalism	Materialism, competition, individualism

Sense of well being	Positively consistent despite appearances due to relationship w/source	In constant flux and struggle
Life space	Infinite and unlimited (spiritual manifesting)	Finite and limited (beginning w/birth, ending w/death)
Perspective	Holistic/oneness	Segmented, fragmented (duality)
Peace, happiness orientation	Eternal	Temporal (temporary)
Stress, anxiety orientation	Carefree	Continual confrontation
Love orientation	Unconditional (see beyond truth)	Conditional (focus on appearance)
Interpersonal relationships	Manifestation of sharing spiritual union	Manifestation of material attraction
Group orientation	Unity through ideology	Unity through common goals or specific aim

AFRICENTRIC SOCIALIZATION

Paradigm for The Positive Development
of
Black People

RECOMMENDED READING

CHAPTER ONE-ENDANGERED
AFRICAN AMERICAN MEN

1. A.F. Poussaint, "What Every Black Woman Should Know About A Black Man" *Ebony* (August 1982) pp. 36-40.
2. Ralph Ellison, *Invisible Man* (New York: Signet, 1980).
3. Richard Wright, *Native Son* (New York: Harper and Row, 1940).
4. Peter Bauer, *Equality, The Third World, and Economic Delusion* (Cambridge MA: Harvard University Press, 1981) p. 88.
5. *Cleveland Plain Dealer*, "Third World Needs Help To Curb Birth Rates" (December 13, 1987) p. A-8.
6. Ibid, p. A-8
7. *Cleveland Plain Dealer*, "U.S. Births To Foreign-Born Rise, Study Says" (January 6, 1987) p. A-4.

8. Franklin Thomas, Speaker, "The New Demographics," Annual Dinner of The Joint Center For Political Studies, Washington, D.C., March 26, 1986.

9. Frances Cress Welsing, M.D., "AIDS: A Man-Made Disease," *The Black American*, 27:46, (November 12-18, 1987) p. 21.

10. William Raspberry, "Detroit Is A City Of Children's Funerals," *Cleveland Plain Dealer* (May 1, 1987) p. B-9.

11. Ben Primm, *AIDS: A Special Report, The State Of Black America*, 1987, National Urban League, p. 159.

12. U.S. Center For Disease Control, *AIDS Among Blacks and Hispanics, Morbidity And Mortality*, Atlanta, 1986, p. 655.

13. National Institute On Alcohol Abuse And Alcoholism (NIAAA), *A Guide To Planning Alcoholism Treatment Programs* (HHS, Pub., 1986) p. 57.

14. Robert Paynter, "Introduction to Alcohol Comes Early For Ghetto Kids," *Akron Beacon Journal* (August 24, 1987) p. A-8.

15. Commission On Racial Justice, "Toxic Wastes And Race In The United States," United Church Of Christ, 1987, pp. 18-19.

16. "Showdown At Sunrise," *Essence* (July 1991) p. 55.

17. Herb Goldberg, *Hazards Of Being Male* (New York: Signet, 1976) pp. 43-44.

18. Molefi Asante, *Afrocentricity* (New Jersey: Africa World Press, 1988).

19. James L. Myers, *Understanding An Afro-Centric World View: Introduction To An Optimal Psychology* (Dubuque, IA: Kendall/Hunt, 1988).

20. Leon Chestang, *Character Development In A*

Hostile Society (Chicago: University of Chicago Press, 1972): p. 2.

CHAPTER TWO-THE DETERIORATION OF AFRICAN AMERICAN MEN

1. Jawanza Kunjufu, *Countering The Conspiracy To Destroy Black Boys Vol. II* (Chicago: African American Images, 1984) p. 10.
2. *Newsweek,* "The Drug Gangs," (March 23, 1988) p. 20.
3. Useni Eugene Perkins, *Explosion Of Black Chicago Street Gangs 1900 To Present* (Chicago: Third World Press, (1987) p. 38.
4. National Urban League Research Department, *Fact Sheet: The Black Male,* Washington, D.C., March 1988.
5. Samuel F. Yette, *The Choice: The Issue Of Black Male Survival* (Berkley: 1971) p. 14.
6. Peter F. Drucker, *The New Society* (New York: Harper & Brothers, 1949) p. 199.
7. Frederick Douglass, *The Life And Writings Of Frederick Douglass,* Philip S. Foner, Ed. (New York: International Publisher, 1955): Vol II p. 224.
8. Franklin A. Thomas, Speaker, "New Demographics", Annual Dinner of The Joint Center For Political Studies, Washington March 26, 1986.
9. U.S. Department Of Labor, *Workforce 2000* (Indianapolis, IN: Hudson Institute, 1987) p. 102.
10. Baker, Carpenter, Amico, Kim, Morgan, Wielgosz, A Report On The National Longitudinal Surveys Of Youth Labor Market Experience In 1982, *Pathways To The Future* (Worthington,

OH: Ohio State University Center For Human Resource Research: ED. 261107 1984) Vol IV.

11. Office Of Research And Improvement, *Dealing With Dropouts: The Urban Superintendents' Call To Action* (U.S. Department of Education: November 1987) p. 1.
12. *Vital Statistics Of the United States, 1970-1975* (Washington, D.C.: U.S. Government Printing Office, 1975). Tables 1-26.
13. Seiden, loc. cit.
14. Herbert Gutman, *The Black Family In Slavery And Freedom 1750-1925* (New York: Pantheon, 1976).
15. William Strickland,"Where Have All The Heroes Gone?", *Essence* (November 1985) p. 76.
16. Richard Seiden, "We're Driving Young Blacks To Suicide," *Psychology Today* (August 1970) pp. 24-28.
17. *Vital Statistics Of The United States, 1970-1975.*
18. U.S. Department of Labor, *Workforce 2000* (Indianapolis, IN: Hudson Institute, 1987) p xxi.
19. Robert Staples, *Black Masculinity* (San Francisco, CA: Black Scholar Press, 1984) p. 65.
20. Emile Durkeim, *Suicide* (Glencoe, IL: The Free Press, 1952).
21. Warren Breed, "The Negro And Fatalistic Suicide," *Pacific Sociological Review* 13 (Summer 1970) pp. 156-162.
22. James Baldwin, *The Fire Next Time* (New York: Dial Press, 1963) p. 19.

CHAPTER THREE-CULTIVATING A NEW HARVEST OF MEN

1. *Essence* (November 1985) p. 72.
2. Gloria Naylor, *The Women Of Brewster Place*

(New York: Penguin, 1982).

3. Yehudi A. Cohen, "Ceremonies In The Second Stage Of Puberty," In *Childhood To Adolescence: Legal Systems And Taboos* (Chicago: Aldine Publishing Company, 1964).

4. Maulana Karenga, *Kawaida Theory* (Inglewood, CA:Kawaida Publications, 1980).

5. Wade Nobles, *The Black Family And Its Children: The Survival Of Humanness* (Unpublished paper).

6. Janice Hale, *Black Children: Their Roots, Culture And Learning Styles* (Provo, UT: Brigham Young University Press, 1982).

7. Jawanza Kunjufu, *Critical Issues in Educating African American Youth* (Chicago: African American Images, 1989) pp. 35-40.

CHAPTER FOUR-AFRICENTRICITY:
A NEW WAY OF LIFE

1. Signithia Fordham, "Racclessness as a Factor in Black Students' School Success: Pragmatic Strategy or Pyrrhic Victory," *Harvard Educational Review*, Reprint Series No. 21, Cambridge, MA, 1990, p. 233.

2. Beckwith Saitoti, *Maasai* (New York: Harry Abrams, Inc., 1990) p. 184.

3. Ray Raphael, *The Men From The Boys* (Lincoln, NE, London: University Of Nebraska Press) p. 195.

4. Nsenga Warfield-Coppock, *Africentric Theory and Applications,Volume I: Adolescent Rites Of Passage* (Washington, D.C.: Baobab, 1940) p. 135.